D1304443

the BLACK SWAN effect

A Response to Gender Hierarchy in the Church

FELICITY DALE

Peggy Batcheller-Hijar, Neil Cole, Jan Diss, Katie Driver,

Dave Ferguson, Michael Frost, Alan Hirsch, Suzette Lambert, Floyd

McClung, Julie Ross, Frank Viola, Jon Zens

FOREWORD BY LYNNE HYBELS

KINGDOM ♥ HEART

P U B L I S H I N G

The Black Swan Effect:
A Response to Gender Hierarchy in the Church

This book is dedicated to all the "black swans" who have gone before us—women from the pages of history, from every conceivable church background—who serve as our examples, and to the Baraks who have opened doors for them and cheered them on.

ACKNOWLEDGEMENTS

The Black Swan Effect has been a team effort from start to finish. During the course of several years, our team of women (Felicity Dale, Peggy Batcheller-Hijar, Jan Diss, Katie Driver, Suzette Lambert, and Julie Ross) amassed hours of conversation around the topic of women in ministry before deciding God was calling us to write a book that would impact the conversation about gender bias in the church. The book you hold in your hands is the result. While all of us contributed our ideas throughout, the introduction and epilogue were the work of Jan Diss and Felicity Dale. Julie Ross was responsible for the majority of the vignettes. Felicity coordinated the project—compiling submissions from contributing authors, writing the introductions to each chapter, and overseeing the details.

The men who have contributed (Neil Cole, Dave Ferguson, Michael Frost, Alan Hirsch, Floyd McClung, Frank Viola, and Jon Zens) have done far more than submit a chapter. Not only do they promote women in their own situations, they have encouraged our team of women and cheered us on—willing to stand with us, to promote us, and to "have our backs." Our thanks to each of them.

Lynne Hybels lent us her wisdom and influence in writing the foreword.

Thanks are due to others as well. Leslie Kim was part of all the initial women's conversations. Ross Rohde and Marty Folsom deserve special mention, as do Erik and Jen Fish. The readers of Felicity's blog (simplychurch.com) have helped shape our thinking during the years with their insightful questions and comments. Others have sent us articles and references. You know who you are.

THE BLACK SWAN EFFECT

"As the Western Church wrestles with regaining its missional impulse, *The Black Swan Effect* provides a launching point for timely conversations within individual congregations and faith communities. No matter what side of the issue you find yourself on, this book is an invaluable read. Seek God and read with a willingness to grow and this book will challenge you and your church to partner with Jesus on mission to be more effective in Gospel ministry."

Justin Meier | President, Creekwood Church Consulting
Church Expansion Strategist for the Churches of God General Conference

"Once again, Felicity has done the rest of us a great service. In *The Black Swan Effect,* she has assembled a group of men and women who write powerfully on this important subject—God doesn't place limits on women. Questions about troubling biblical texts are clearly addressed. Stories of remarkable women (the 'black swans') throughout history and today help us visualize what can be in the future. I'll be recommending this book to all of our house church leaders."

John White | Leadership Team, LK10 Community (Lk10.com)

"The holy winds of change are gusting up all over the globe as women break free from the grip of gender inequality. This book is like a manifesto of liberty that will crush the lies that have kept women sidelined for too long. *The Black Swan Effect* is a prophetic collective of writers who don't just talk about the injustice of sexism, but who are each committed to helping dismantle it. Read it and be inspired."

Pam Hogeweide | Author, *Unladylike*

"If 'black swan' logic makes what you don't know sometimes even more relevant than what you do know, then this book could equally have been entitled, *The Church's Black Death,* so tragic have been the consequences from the muted voices and squashed visions of women in the history of the church. Here is a clarion call for a New Reformation encompassing the whole body of Christ."

Leonard Sweet | Best-selling Author, Professor
(Drew University, George Fox University), and Chief Contributor to sermons.com

"What we believe affects how we act. If what we believe is incorrect, it will lead to poor behavior. *The Black Swan Effect* graciously addresses how incorrect understanding has led to behavior that wounds Christian women and the Kingdom of God. *The Black Swan Effect* should be read by everyone who cares about our sisters in Christ and God's Kingdom."

Ross Rohde | Author, *Viral Jesus*

"With theological, historical, and practical insight, this book will help shift the reader into a new way of thinking. I believe that women will be inspired to move past the hurdles that have kept them from obeying God in ministry leadership while helping them through the internal changes they may have to make in the process."

Joy Strang | CFO/COO, *Charisma Media*

"Felicity has done an incredible job of tackling the very thorny issue of women leadership in the church. The biblical material, the insights and experience of multiple contributors, and the testimonies of female leaders make this book one of the best I have read on this issue. I pray this book will unfetter the hearts and minds of leaders everywhere so that the full potential of Kingdom leadership, both male and female, will be reached."

David Watson | Vice President for Global Disciple-Making, Cityteam Ministries

"In *The Black Swan Effect*, Felicity and a multiplicity of male and female contributors powerfully disclose the true role of women in the body of Christ. Real-life examples and biblically grounded teachings guide both men and women to honor each other as equals, help churches move toward balanced male-female leadership teams, and reveal the correct interpretation of those passages of Scripture that seem to limit women's role in the Church. Anyone wishing to discover a golden egg of truth that will liberate us all into a new dimension of unity and teamwork for God's Kingdom absolutely must read *The Black Swan Effect*."

Leanna Cinquanta | TellAsia Ministries (tellasia.org)

"The single most important issue facing the body of Christ when it comes to being serious about fulfilling the Great Commission may be changing our mindset about women in leadership. *The Black Swan Effect* is an anthem for releasing a worldwide movement of men and women to disciple the nations. If you want a fresh encounter with the heart of God and the depth of wisdom in the Scriptures and God's redemptive plan, this book is for you. *The Black Swan Effect* will challenge you; it might offend you; it may just set you free."

Erik Fish | Student CPX; Author, *Disciple: Journey with Jesus. Change Your World*

"God had to give Peter three visions before he got the clue that he fully welcomes Gentiles. Christ has given the church men *and women* apostles, prophets, evangelists, pastors and teachers. Each chapter in this book is a vision, so don't be surprised if God gives you a kairos moment (a divine moment that shapes our destiny), when you start to appreciate and value women in the same way he does. Let the black swan revolution begin!"

JR Woodward | National Director of the V3 Church Planting Movement
Author, *Creating a Missional Culture*

Anj Riffel of Kingdom Heart Publishing is responsible for editing and design. Hers is the genius behind the cover. She's not just creatively gifted, she's been a delight to work with too. Together with Michelle Booth, they've greatly improved the way the book reads.

Various authors have gone before us and made our way easier. Special thanks to theologian Philip B. Payne for his scholarly book, *Man and Woman: One in Christ,* which has been a reference book on many an occasion, and to Loren Cunningham and David Hamilton for *Why Not Women: A Biblical Study of Women in Missions, Ministry, and Leadership*—a book that gave several of us hope when all seemed bleak for women.

Finally, we want to acknowledge our spouses and families who have put up with our preoccupation with this topic. They've listened to our rants and theories, been patient with our endless stories of injustice, and above all, have encouraged and promoted us at every step. We are blessed!

TABLE OF CONTENTS

FOREWORD
GOD, WHAT IS MINE TO DO?

By Lynne Hybels

Nearly four decades ago, my husband and I planted a church in a movie theater. From those humble beginnings, God has multiplied our ministry beyond our wildest imagination. I'm grateful for the opportunity I've had to travel and meet women who challenge and inspire me to walk more closely with Jesus. I'm also grateful to serve in a church where the future belongs to young leaders who are free to lead and follow and serve and pray without thought to gender-defined rules and roles.

We have often been criticized by those who believe our commitment to gift-based serving rather than gender-based hierarchy is a denial of Scripture and a capitulation to culture. I don't believe that is true, though I do admit that a bit of youthful naiveté shaped our attitude toward women in ministry.

In the early 70s, my then boyfriend (now husband), Bill, was teaching a Bible study for high school students in a church basement. As more and more students began to attend, it was necessary to divide the students into smaller groups for accountability and deeper relationships. Each group needed a leader, so we chose the most mature and competent students, many of whom were young women. In time, an unexpected thing happened. Parents of our high school students began attending the Bible study and asked us to start a similar gathering for adults. By then, many of the students we had identified as leaders in the high school ministry were twentysomethings looking for a new adventure, so they joined us and became leaders in the newly planted church.

As the church grew, so did the responsibilities handled by these young leaders—both men and women. And then the questions started. Well actually, it was just one question, repeated over and over: "Why do you let women lead?" Why? Because when we needed leaders we looked for people who demonstrated strong relational skills, stellar character, a deep commitment to God, and proven leadership skills. Many of the people who best fit those criteria were women. We didn't let them lead. We asked them to lead. We needed them.

Okay, so women can lead. But should they? The question then became, "What's your biblical rationale?" We didn't have a ready answer for that, so our church's new elders—which included women—began an 18-month study of the issue under the leadership of Dr. Gilbert Bilezikian, then a New Testament professor at Wheaton college. Eventually, Dr. "B" published the findings of that study in his book, *Beyond Sex Roles: What the Bible Says About A Woman's Place in Church and Family*, which argues for gift-based, rather than gender-based, participation in all of life, including the church. That has been our position at Willow Creek Community Church for almost 40 years. We can't imagine our church without strong, kind, competent, grace-filled women and men using their gifts with equal freedom in children's ministry and on the board of directors, in pastoring small groups and in preaching Sunday sermons. Male staff members at Willow must demonstrate a willingness to be co-laborers with women, and to serve under the leadership of women.

Growing up in this environment gave our daughter, Shauna Niequist, the freedom to discover, pursue, and enjoy her true gifts and passions. Now a thirtysomething author and speaker, she has been shocked to discover that many of her peers—intelligent, energetic, gifted, godly young women—had and are having a very different experience. Bill and I are shocked too, that these young women are still fighting a battle to be seen and heard, to be valued and released for service in their churches.

Why do I feel strongly about this issue? It's not because I'm an angry feminist with a chip on my shoulder due to denied opportunities. It's not because I wanted to lead or teach and was told I couldn't. Frankly, my experience has been just the opposite. For most of my life, I haven't wanted to be a "public person" in ministry. In fact, I have at times actively resisted the platform offered me, not because I'm a woman, but because I'm a wounded, fearful, and insecure person (probably more than you needed to know!). In more recent years, I've made peace with my public role, but I still battle fears and a sense of inadequacy. It is only a deep sense of calling that pushes me into public ministry. Even so, when I often find myself the only woman sitting around a table with men in dark suits talking about theology or international development or peacemaking, I think, *How did I get here?*

So why am I writing these words? Because my meandering ministry path has put me in proximity to so much brokenness and pain: human trafficking, extreme poverty, war, gender-based violence, and displacement. In all these areas of brokenness, I've seen women suffer so severely. But I've also seen their resilience, their strength, their unflagging commitment to God, to their families, to their communities, and to the future. I've become convinced that women are the greatest untapped resource in the world. Their voices need to be heard. Their wisdom needs to be sought. Their compassionate action needs to be valued. Their skills need to be seen and honed and honored.

Why am I writing these words? Because I look forward to a time beyond the gender debates, when women can pray a simple prayer: "God, what is mine to do?" And when they sense God's answer—perhaps an unexpected answer—they will have to pray for courage, wisdom, and steadfastness in order to be faithful to that call. But they won't have to wonder if they're hearing correctly. They won't have wonder if it's okay for a woman to answer that call. They will be free to get to work for God's Kingdom.

And the amazing women and men who wrote the chapters in this book can be their guides along the way.

PREFACE

THE STORY BEHIND THE BOOK

By Felicity Dale

"The Lord reminded me of the story of Deborah and Barak. Can we read it together?"

Twelve women were gathered in our living room. We had come together for a weekend to seek God about the role of women in the church. Through the years, we have learned that God loves to speak to his people corporately. Each of us had spent time alone seeking his direction before bringing our contributions to the group. The Lord reminded Peggy, one of our members, of this passage in Judges 4 and 5—a beautiful story of victory as men and women cooperate together.

> Deborah, the wife of Lappidoth, was a prophet who was judging Israel at that time. She would sit under the Palm of Deborah, between Ramah and Bethel in the hill country of Ephraim, and the Israelites would go to her for judgment. One day she sent for Barak son of Abinoam, who lived in Kedesh in the land of Naphtali. She said to him, 'This is what the Lord, the God of Israel, commands you: Call out 10,000 warriors from the tribes of Naphtali and Zebulun at Mount Tabor. And I will call out Sisera, commander of Jabin's army, along with his chariots and warriors, to the Kishon River. There I will give you victory over him.' Barak told her, 'I will go, but only if you go with me.' (Judg. 4:4–8)

As a group of women, we longed to see the prevailing attitude of the church change toward women. But what impact could a small group have on centuries of tradition? We certainly didn't want to act out of a wrong attitude—as a reaction to perceived injustice—yet we were sensing a groundswell, a change of opinion about the role of women across the body of Christ. The Holy Spirit is up to something.

God spoke to us through the story of Deborah and Barak; we were not to go it alone. A group of women trying to change the status quo, no matter how gently we approached the subject, could be seen as militant feminists—griping about the way we've been treated and grasping for our rights. But if men stood with us, it could become something much bigger with greater impact, part of a Kingdom movement that could multiply the harvest. Involving men would not just add validity; it could serve to grant both genders permission to pursue the path of championing women to do and be everything God intends. Also, most men are typically more likely to listen to other men.

But let me back up a little.

The role of a woman in leadership in the body of Christ can be a lonely one. While she may have many friends, she often has few female peers. The leaders around her tend to be male, and Christian tradition often dictates it inappropriate for her to develop deep friendships with the opposite gender outside of marriage.

Five years ago, recognizing a need for peer fellowship, I reached out to a few women who play a significant role in the body of Christ—each a leader with influence that goes way beyond her local church. We enjoyed regular fellowship via conference calls from different parts of the country.

As our fellowship grew deeper, a natural discussion topic was the role of women in the church. While many women (and men) are content with the status quo and have no desire to see change (we must each follow as the Lord leads), each of us knew women who desire everything God has for them, but yet hang back, waiting for a man to take the lead. What could we do to give them permission to follow the Holy Spirit no matter where he led, even if it meant taking the initiative? How could we encourage men to stand with them?

We knew from our own experience that the church in the West, with notable exceptions, has historically sidelined and marginalized women. Because they've been taught that they're stepping out of line if they initiate or lead, some women have settled into passivity. Men lead; women follow. The mission of Jesus suffers as a large portion of the workforce for the harvest waits for men to take the initiative.

On a few occasions, our team of women went away together for several days of prayer and fellowship. We always returned to the idea that God longs to free women to fulfill their destinies—that if they were released, the workforce for God's Kingdom could potentially double.

This all led up to the weekend God spoke to us about Deborah and Barak. The cooperation they displayed encouraged us to approach a few male allies who shared our beliefs. They pledged to stand with us. Together, we would seek to release women from the bonds held in place by fear of change and misinterpretation of God's Word.

Many men actively advocate on behalf of women. Some take every opportunity to speak about the injustice that exists in the church and do everything they can to promote women. Others have made the study of Scriptures concerning women a priority. Still others take practical steps to hold the doors open, allowing women to pursue their calling to ministry.

When we made the decision to write a book together, we asked several men from different church backgrounds to contribute. They agreed to share from their particular areas of interest and expertise. We are so grateful to them for their willingness to identify with us and actively champion the cause of women.

The conversation about gender is rapidly gaining traction in church circles. It's as though the Holy Spirit is firing up interest across the church spectrum. This isn't a move of angry women trying to right the wrongs of the past. It's a rising tide of both men and women who long to see God's mission on earth accomplished, and who recognize that God himself is fulfilling his Word:

There is neither Jew nor Gentile, neither slave nor free, nor is there male and female, for you are all one in Christ Jesus. (Gal. 3:28, NIV)

Could this be one of the next major moves of God? Could the release of women into the Kingdom workforce help to usher in the end-time harvest?

Here is what we hope to accomplish through this book:

1. To present a vision for what can happen as men and women work together for the sake of the harvest.

2. To give women permission and inspiration to follow the Lord— to reach their full potential and help other women do the same.

3. To encourage men to welcome women as equal co-laborers in the Kingdom, standing with them as they fulfill God's calling on their lives.

4. To equip both men and women to bring an informed and positive contribution to the increasingly crucial conversation on gender within the church.

Note to readers:

*Proceeds from this book will go toward
training women church planters in developing nations
and helping victims of sex trafficking.*

Chapter introductions were written by Felicity Dale.

INTRODUCTION

THE TIMES THEY ARE A-CHANGIN'

By Jan Diss and Felicity Dale

Paradigm Shifts and Theological Interpretation

When Martin Luther nailed his *Ninety-Five Theses* to the door of Wittenberg Cathedral in 1517, he made countless people aware of what the Bible said about grace. His theses could be quickly printed and distributed to the masses because of the recent invention of moveable type. This new interpretation of Scripture produced one of history's most profound paradigm shifts—the Protestant Reformation.

Why did it take 1,500 years for a large portion of the church to read the Bible in this light, not only believing *all* had sinned and fallen short of the glory of God, but also discovering grace is a gift from God? For many who read the Bible today, the concept is plain. But prior to Luther, most people believed they had to earn or purchase their salvation.

There are other times in history when the Christian world has misinterpreted the Bible. One classic example is the Copernican Revolution. In 1543, Copernicus wrote a treatise called *On the Revolution of the Heavenly Spheres*. It completely challenged the existing idea of a geocentric model of the universe in which the sun was seen as revolving around the earth. Copernicus proposed the heliocentric view that the earth revolves around the sun. In 1616, the Roman Catholic Church banned Copernicus' book and any other work that either defended a sun-centric view of the world or attempted to reconcile this view with the Bible. In 1633, Galileo was convicted of heresy for supporting Copernicus' position and was placed under house arrest for the remainder of his life. It wasn't until 1835 (almost three centuries after Copernicus' original proposition) that the church finally repented. In other words, there was a time when everyone *knew* for certain that the earth was the center of the universe. Anything else was heresy. And then there came a time when everyone knew the exact opposite was true.

Similarly, there was a time in United States when the Bible was used to defend slavery, and there came a time when Scripture was re-examined and understood to convey the worth and equality of each person created in God's image. Those most resistant to change their views were people whose lives were invested in the status quo—much like the Post Medieval Catholic Church was the most affected by the schism resulting from Martin Luther's presentation of grace as a gift from God that could not be bought, sold, or earned.

And how about the issue of God's supernatural power? In the modern era of church history, many Christians, enamored with the scientific revolution, abandoned belief in a God who performs miracles and heals people. Today, many have reclaimed this belief in light of evidence from around the world that God continues to answer prayer in extraordinary and inexplicable ways.

As we can see, there is a precedent for Christians rereading Scripture with new eyes to find God's truth for their generation. It has happened before in truly significant ways. What if this is God's prescribed time for his children to re-examine the Bible regarding the role of women? Who has a vested interest in things staying the same? There have been times when everyone knew God did not want women to lead in the church. Could there be a time when everyone knows the opposite is true?

Lance Wallnau offers a fascinating YouTube video called "Piercing the Veil."[1] The basic concept suggests that once you reach critical mass on a revelation, everyone easily gains access to what was once contested territory. The role of women is contested territory in many Christian circles. But what if this is all about to change? A whole generation could arise who has only known freedom for men and women to serve together equally in the body of Christ.

It Only Takes One: The Black Swan Effect

The term "black swan" was common in sixteenth century London. Everyone *knew* swans were white, and black swans presumably did not exist, so the term came to mean something farfetched, not real. However, in 1636, a Dutch explorer discovered nomadic, red-billed black swans in Western Australia. All of a sudden, black swans were no longer an impossibility, and the meaning of the term changed from something farfetched to something once thought of as farfetched, but now known as reality.[2]

> In English, when the phrase was coined, the black swan was presumed not to exist. The importance of the simile lies in its analogy to the fragility of any system of thought. A set of conclusions is potentially undone once any of its fundamental postulates is disproved. In this case, the observation of a single black swan would be the undoing of the phrase's underlying logic, as well as any reasoning that followed from that underlying logic.[3]

Today, there is a well-known species of black swans. All it took was one swan to change people's minds forever.

In 1954, British runner Roger Bannister proved it only took one person to break the goal of a four-minute mile. Athletes had been attempting to break the four-minute barrier for years, and it was said to be a physical impossibility for the human body. Enter Bannister, a runner who was training to be a physician. Prior to starting his running career at Oxford University in 1946, Bannister had never worn spikes, or even run on a track—but he quickly showed such promise that he was selected as an Olympic hopeful. Bannister came in fourth place in the one-mile race at the 1952 Olympics. As other athletes inched towards the four-minute goal, Bannister, too, set his sights on the record.

The fateful event took place at a running meet in Oxford on May 6, 1954, watched by about 3,000 spectators. Bannister won the race. The announcer spun out the results as long as possible:

Ladies and gentlemen, here is the result of event nine, the one-mile: First, number 41, R.G. Bannister, Amateur Athletic Association and formerly of Exeter and Merton Colleges, Oxford, with a time which is a new meeting and track record, and which—subject to ratification—will be a new English Native, British National, All-Comers, European, British Empire and World Record. The time was 3... [4]

The remainder of the announcement was impossible to hear as a roar went up from the crowd. Bannister's time was 3 minutes, 59.4 seconds. The four-minute barrier had been broken. Once Bannister proved it could be done, many other athletes subsequently broke the four-minute barrier and it became the new standard for male professional middle-distance runners. Amazingly, the record has since been lowered by almost 17 seconds.

Why then, does much of the church world dismiss biblical examples like Deborah, the prophetess/judge who presided over Israel for 40 years?[5] Why is it considered an anomaly that a church met in Lydia's home, Junia was an apostle,[6] a group of women were the first to see and announce that Jesus had risen from the dead,[7] or that Queen Esther saved her people? These remarkable women are often relegated to the sidelines by commentators who say they were exceptions, not normative, or not the standard God has for women. But all it takes is one example—one black swan—to know, by the grace of God, a thing exists. And if there is one, there could be many.

The Bible is full of stories about courageous women who, even in pre-Dark Age cultures, demonstrated leadership and were used mightily by God. This book, too, is filled with vignettes—stories about ordinary women with no titles, positions, or salaries, and yet they are wise teachers, capable church starters, and Jesus-loving activists who make a difference in their worlds. We've also included stories of women who, like Roger Bannister, have broken through barriers and are more widely known for their contributions. All of them belong to a breed of beautiful, courageous black swans.

Tipping Points

Every breakthrough concept has a tipping point—a trigger point where the foreshadowing of an idea, trend, attitude, behavior, or direction becomes a mainstream reality.[8] Two ways of considering tipping points are pertinent here. First, there are societal tipping points, which indicate that critical mass has been achieved and change is real. Second, there are personal tipping points, which occur when individuals become ready to accept the new societal norm.

Much of the Western world has now passed the societal tipping point on issues related to women in leadership positions of government, business, medicine, education, and other realms. While the whole of the social order has not changed in the West, it has reached a point of no return regarding women in these roles. There will not be fewer female government officials, business owners, or PhDs in the next generation—there will likely be more.

However, the personal tipping point in reference to a woman's role in the church has not yet occurred—except, perhaps, in a few mainline denominations. While people who follow Jesus and love his Word should never change their views based on popular opinions, societal trends can make individual Christians stop, think, pray, and reread Scripture with fresh eyes and hearts. Sometimes, in doing so, God removes blinders and awakens the hearts of his people in new ways.

Harajuku is a neighborhood in Tokyo where young people come to express themselves through fashion. A Harajuku Moment—according to author Tim Ferriss[9]—describes a personal tipping point when individuals experience an awakening and make dramatic shifts to improve their well-being. Is it time for a Harajuku Moment in the body of Christ? This book is intended to help both men and women seek the heart of God as they consider making personal shifts in their attitudes, beliefs, and behaviors related to the role of women in the church.

Indicators of Change?

A groundswell is rising that could become one of the next waves of the Holy Spirit. Someday, the idea that women are created for only subservient roles will seem as outdated as the notion of slavery. This book is written in an age when the church in the West is in crisis—it is losing membership, baptisms are declining, denominations are shrinking, and Christian values are no longer normative. What if an enhanced understanding of the role of women could help the church thrive again? Any study of major revivals will show that women play vital roles in the prayer, evangelism, social reform, church planting, and societal transformation that always coincide with revival. Here are just a few examples:

- Author/preacher Phoebe Palmer, sometimes called the "mother" of the holiness movement, was the best-known woman in the American Methodist Church in the nineteenth century, when that denomination was the largest evangelical group in the United States.

- Dorothy Sun presently co-directs the China division of Christian Aid Mission, which trains missionaries and has started Bible schools in every province of China. Some say the revival in China is the largest in history, with 30,000 people becoming followers of Jesus every day.

- Christian social reformer, scholar, activist, and evangelist, Pandita Ramabai, was an orphan who God used to facilitate a great outpouring of his Spirit among women and girls in a revival in Mukti, India.

- At the turn of the twentieth century, God used Methodist missionary Mary Culler White and Presbyterian missionary Louise Hoard McCully to start a prayer meeting in Korea, which began to spread and was the precursor to revival.

- Female converts of the revival movement are starting and leading churches in India, China, Korea, and many other countries.

The generation to witness the final end-time harvest will be a fully functioning church, where there is neither Jew nor Greek, slave nor free, male nor female—unity, not division. Why not today? The church has two main options. She can continue as she is—a church that puts great focus on attracting not-yet-believers; a church where women (and men) are being sidelined, becoming disillusioned, and leaving en masse, taking their families with them. Or, the church can become missional—in which case women play a vital role.

Missional versus Attractional

Only a few short years ago (and still today, in many churches), most of us assumed that church is supposed to be attractional in nature—people become Christians when someone invites them to a presentation of the Gospel and they respond to an invitation to know Jesus. While we thank God for the many whose lives have been transformed in this way, there is a new recognition that Jesus himself demonstrated other ways of reaching out to people.[10]

It is far more effective for the body of Christ to be missional in outlook. Rather than inviting people to our meetings where we listen to one or two specially trained ministers, all believers are sent out to act as ambassadors of the Kingdom. We represent our King at work, in our neighborhoods—any place where our lives interact with others. If we bring a new believer into our church, we have made a single disciple. On the other hand, if we reach out to that person's circle of influence in a way that's familiar and comfortable, we potentially win a community for Christ. This missional pattern of Kingdom living needs all of us, both men and women, to be available for the harvest. We can no longer be mere spectators.

Here in the States, we are now less churched than we have ever been.[11] If we are to see a turnaround in the current trends, we need every available worker for the harvest—of both genders. What might happen if the current church leadership encouraged women to initiate Kingdom ventures, to reach out to their unbelieving friends, start churches, contribute to missions strategy, teach and train others—co-laboring alongside them as equal partners in the work of the Kingdom?

A movement of "black swans"—women embracing their freedom and everything God intends for them—could release a flood of others, who currently sit passively in the pews, to follow their example.

Time for a Personal Paradigm Shift?

Is it possible, since you are reading this book, that you are on the verge of a paradigm shift of your own? Perhaps you sense the world changing around you. Perhaps you are reading the Bible with a new set of eyes and wondering about some of the difficult passages about women. Maybe this is your personal Harajuku Moment.

If you are like most Christians we know, one of three primary motivations propels you into this discussion about women in ministry: mission, theology, or justice.

MISSION: Many Christians—both men and women—have come to the conclusion that there is no better way to double the size of God's missions workforce and to hasten the day of Kingdom-come than to fully deploy women to use their spiritual gifts and God-given capacities. These are missional men and women who believe our God is a God who sends, and the Great Commission is meant as a command for every follower of Christ. Women are already some of the most productive missions leaders in their churches, but what if—in addition to studying about missions, praying for missions, and giving to missions offerings—each of these female leaders learned how she was wired by God to activate missions both locally and globally?

THEOLOGY: Others are asking theological questions. They are investigating how the Bible portrays women, especially women leaders. Were the New Testament writers—in particular, the Apostle Paul—misogynists? Are there alternative interpretations for some of the really difficult passages of Scripture? People who approach the subject from a theological perspective study the Bible seriously, and may have been taught to translate it in a way that seems to subjugate women. But many are currently questioning this doctrine.

JUSTICE: Still others who enter this discussion are drawn to it because of issues related to justice and human dignity. They want to know why some religions undermine the worth of women, why many churches are not equal opportunity employers, and why Christians are not engaging more with issues such as sex trafficking, global female infanticide, spousal abuse, or uneven gender-based pay scales. As they study Scripture, they are assured that God creates all men and women in his image, and they can't even imagine a God who would discriminate against women.

This book addresses each of these three themes from multiple authors and perspectives. Most of the author-contributors have considered all three angles, even if they major on only one of them here. Some have had their own Harajuku Moments. They have daughters who love Jesus but struggle to find their place in the church. They have experienced cultures where women wear veils or young girls have no access to education. Our female contributors offer first-hand experience of being in situations where their good ideas and worthy contributions were either ignored or stolen. We hope their experiences serve to motivate, nourish, fortify, and release you.

May the tribe of black swans increase and freely serve their King!

Discussion Questions

1. Do you believe any roles in the church are gender-specific?

2. In many churches, women are limited to teaching children, women's ministry, etc. Does this come from Scripture? From tradition?

3. Which of your gender paradigms are you willing to have challenged through this book?

Introduction Notes

1. "Piercing the Veil," Lance Wallnau, *YouTube,* January 2011,
   http://bit.ly/V61mrR.

2. "The Black Swan (2007 book)," *Wikipedia,* accessed October 2013,
   http://en.wikipedia.org/wiki/The_Black_Swan_(2007_book);
   "Australian Black Swan Facts," accessed October 2013,
   http://www.svswans.com/black.html; "Black Swan Theory," *Wikipedia,*
   accessed October 2013, http://en.wikipedia.org/wiki/Black_swan_theory.

3. "The Black Swan (2007 book)," *Wikipedia.*

4. Ibid.

5. Judges 4–5.

6. Romans 16:7.

7. Matthew 28:1–10; Mark 16:9–11; Luke 24:1–10; John 20:11–19.

8. The term "tipping point" was popularized by Malcolm Gladwell in his book
   of the same name.

9. The idea is taken from his book, *The 4-Hour Body.*

10. The story of Jesus sending out the 70 disciples in Luke 10:1–9 is
    one example.

11. According to the book, the *American Church in Crisis* by David T. Olson,
    in America, 3,500–4,000 churches close their doors each year. Balanced
    against this is the number of church starts. From 2000–2005, there was a
    net growth of 303 churches per year (closures combined with new church
    starts). This sounds great until you realize that we need to gain 3,205 per
    year just to keep up with population growth. We are less "churched" now
    than we've ever been. In the average year, half of all churches do not add
    one member through conversion growth.

PART ONE

THE VITAL ROLE
OF WOMEN
IN JESUS' MISSION

BY AGE 15, Leanna Cinquanta was an equestrian champion. She was also a rebellious, proud atheist. God has his ways. In 1986, she had a face-to-face encounter with Jesus that caused her to abandon everything and cast her life at his feet. Later, following two dreams, she bought a one-way ticket to India and founded TellAsia Ministries. Her obedience to an apostolic calling resulted in an incredible church planting movement in the least evangelized and most needy region of northern India. The movement has seen countless lives transformed by the healing, delivering, and saving power of Jesus Christ. Leanna's devotion and willingness to let the Father work through her has given rise to orphanages, humanitarian projects, leadership development, and vocational training. Leanna is small in stature but powerful in his Spirit. She speaks a bold clarion call to step aside from small ambitions into an inheritance of impacting the world for Christ. God can do whatever he wants in a son or daughter who dares to say, "Yes!"

CHAPTER 1

WHY NOT HERE? WHY NOT NOW?

By Floyd McClung

God is using women in extraordinary ways all around the world. Middle-aged housewives in India are training church planters. One was responsible for planting 2,000 churches; the other had planted 6,000. These women, along with countless others, are unsung heroes of the faith.

Author and ministry leader, Floyd McClung,[1] is uniquely positioned to write a chapter about women of great faith. He developed a deep passion for this subject having repeatedly witnessed gifted women, from many cultures and nations, being outright rejected, or more subtly, avoided. Floyd has reached out to the women God brought across his path and championed them in their callings. He served in Youth With a Mission (YWAM) and later co-founded All Nations with his wife, Sally. For more than 20 years, they have discipled women who are now making a difference in the nations.

Worldwide, history is rich with stories—some told, many untold—of brave black swans who stepped forward to answer God's call. Psalm 68 describes a great army of women proclaiming the good news. What could it look like if all women were set free to impact the nations for Christ? What if men and women worked together with that as their goal? God can use women to do mighty works. Why not here? Why not now?

At a recent three-day training event for church leaders, a pastor friend announced, "I don't allow men and women to disciple each other. It's unbiblical!"

As co-leader of the event, I decided not to challenge him publicly, but determined to address the issue later. I was annoyed by the bias of his policy and the assumption that all mature leaders would agree with him. I believe women and men have much to teach each other in discipling relationships, as long as they are above reproach in every regard.

Later that evening, when I asked my friend about his comment, he said emotional entanglement between genders, which could lead to moral compromise, was his main concern. He had seen it happen, all too sadly, on more than one occasion. I agreed with the need for accountability and transparency, but not with turning the need into a policy.

I probed deeper, not willing to allow a good friend to go unchallenged: "You know, Pieter, I was discipled by a woman from New Zealand named Joy Dawson. She was twenty-five years my senior, old enough to be my mother—in fact, she was a spiritual mother to me for many years. Another mother in the Lord, Jean Darnell, mentored me in regard to prophetic ministry in the church. I learned the ways of God from these women—they helped shaped my life. They taught me how to hear God's voice, about spiritual warfare, intercession, the fear of the Lord, and the healthy operation of spiritual gifts in the local church."

I also mentioned instances I knew about women who mentored well-known leaders in the body of Christ, men such as Billy Graham, Bill Bright, Loren Cunningham, and David Yonggi Cho.

"You're right," he said. "I want to teach values, not hand down rules." Pieter looked at me a little sheepishly. Suddenly realizing he had broken this cross-gender mentoring "rule" himself, he confessed, "Now that I think about it, I led my wife to the Lord and discipled her!" We had a good laugh, updated our fellow leaders the next day, and moved on.

As I reflected on our conversation, I wondered whether Pieter had ever sought out the counsel of a godly older woman and whether he would be willing to learn from women. I believed he would. He is a humble man, but out of concern for godliness, he had turned a caution into a rule. This seems to be a common pitfall.

Both Male and Female

To be clear, I believe leaders can be both male and female. Obviously, the church body is comprised of both genders. And certainly, martyrs have been both male and female. Missionaries are both male and female.

But it is important to be more specific, lest we overlook the obvious: both women and men have impacted nations for God because both genders are called by God, and both are given leadership gifts.

I believe leadership in the church is not meant to be gender-specific because, at its core, leadership is about service. It is not about an office or position. Leaders don't serve in order to be leaders; they serve because that's what leaders do. Leaders serve. Period. When we abandon a hierarchical, worldly view of leadership and consider it from this perspective, we can see that both women and men can, and already do, use their gifts to serve—that is, lead.

The church worldwide has been shaped, led, and taught by both men and women—starting in the home, and moving into every sphere of church and public life.

Nation-Impacting Women

I have had the privilege of traveling in 192 countries and have met amazing women in all walks of life. The world knows about Mother Teresa and accepts her radical impact. But what of the tens of thousands of unknown women who are silent heroes of the Kingdom? Take away their service, and the Kingdom of God becomes half or less of what it is today.

I estimate more than 65 percent of the mission force and leadership corps of the church worldwide is female. Serving as Bible translators and church planters, women have opened up unreached people groups to the Gospel, taught men to lead and read, made disciples, trained leaders, and ignited church planting movements.

Some of those same female leaders have subsequently stepped back as second-generation male leaders took charge, watching silently as men went on to take credit for what women had actually done.

A painful example comes to mind. New Life is one of the largest church movements in India today, with thousands of churches throughout the country. I have visited New Life churches in dusty villages, urban slums, and on university campuses. The movement was founded by two couples, including big-hearted Trevor Paterson and his short-but-powerful wife, Isabel. Together, they were an apostolic team; their gifts were complementary.

Isabel's courageous teaching and prophetic gifts helped lay vital foundations for the New Life movement. But years after the movement was founded and Indian leadership took over, the history of the church was rewritten to fit certain leaders' fears and prejudices concerning the role of women. Isabel's role in New Life was hushed up, even denied. Honor was not given to whom honor was due. Indian leaders assumed the duties of overseeing the New Life movement, and then rewrote the history of the movement to ignore the role Isabel had played. Isabel had not demanded recognition, but it had wounded her heart to be ignored, even ostracized, by the very movement she helped found.

Fortunately, through the intervention of the Holy Spirit and loyal friends, this blight was erased from the movement when the senior leader responded to correction from older, godly men who spoke up on Isabel's behalf. Years ago in Mumbai, he humbled himself publicly in the presence of a roomful of leaders, including myself. He asked forgiveness, and in doing so, brought healing to Isabel's heart and set the record straight forever.

New Life churches have transformed several million people's lives. The leaders of this movement have impacted the business, government, education, and arts of the second most populous country in the world. New Life churches are a nation-impacting, transformational movement. And a little lady from Australia helped make it happen!

There are many more stories of women pioneers who impacted nations. Nancy Neville is a tiny general from New Zealand who pioneered the church planting work of Youth With a Mission in Chile, as well as modern missions in the Southern Cone of South America. Nancy is a demure, but powerful woman of God. I watched as macho Chileans and other South Americans conducted leadership schools and missions conferences in the forefront, while their spiritual mother, Nancy, quietly networked, discipled, and led from the back. Such humility is key to the impact of many successful women leaders. They have learned that the secret to leading effectively is to serve, to give up concern about who gets the credit; they just get on with the job.

Another modern church leader I greatly admire is Elizabeth Baumann Cochrane, who pioneered church planting efforts in Nepal at a time when sharing the Gospel was still an imprisonable offense. Liz, in fact, did spend time in prison for her efforts to spread the good news of Jesus. She was fearless in her endeavors. As a result, Nepali believers eventually marched on government buildings, demanding the constitution be changed to recognize the rights of Christians. And it was! Behind the scenes, Liz and others helped pave the way for the major change that took place.

The Surprising Secrets of the World's Largest Church and the World's Fastest Growing Church Planting Movement

Many people have heard of the world's largest church in Seoul, Korea, led by Dr. David Yonggi Cho. What most people do not know is the role Dr. Cho's mother-in-law, Mrs. Choi, played in catalyzing the growth of the church.[2] Mrs. Choi was an outstanding preacher and teacher, and the first of thousands of women who became ministers under Dr. Cho's leadership.

When asked to reveal the secret of his church's growth, Dr. Cho answered, "The key is to release your women!"

We find a similar approach in the world's fastest growing church planting movement, which has reached more than nine million new believers in just 15 years. A few years ago, I asked a key leader how many of the house church leaders in the movement were women. His answer? Close to 70 percent.

What lesson can church leaders learn from these examples? Recognize women leaders! Release your women!

No Hiding Place for This Woman

Corrie ten Boom was a nation-impacting leader in modern Europe. Shortly after the end of World War II, God impressed "Aunt Corrie" to return to Germany, where she had been imprisoned in a concentration camp. She had witnessed her sister's murder at the hand of one the camp guards, so going back to Germany was no small step of obedience. But she obeyed God. Everywhere Aunt Corrie traveled, she preached the Gospel of forgiveness.

My wife, Sally, and I met Aunt Corrie when we were living on a large houseboat called *The Ark* in Amsterdam's main harbor area. It was the height of the Jesus People days in the 1970s, and we were running a halfway house and Christian community for 50 to 60 young street people.

When Aunt Corrie volunteered to speak to our group, she was preparing to go to the United States to make the movie, *The Hiding Place*, and had been invited by Billy Graham to speak to stadiums packed with people. She asked the young Christians on *The Ark* if they would pray for her upcoming visit to America as an evangelist. It was a sight to behold: scores of baby Christians with long hair, tattoos, piercings, and strange hairdos laid hands on Aunt Corrie ten Boom, and commissioned her to preach the good news in the States.

Later, as I walked Aunt Corrie to the car, she confided, "Tomorrow is my birthday. I will be eighty years old."

Surprised, I asked, "What do you want for your birthday?"

With a twinkle in her eye, she replied, "I already bought myself new suitcases! I expect the Lord to give me at least ten more years to travel and preach the Gospel!"

After the time of prayer with the young people on *The Ark,* Aunt Corrie went on to speak to millions of people. Many had read her life story in the book, *The Hiding Place,* and nine million people saw the movie during its first five months.

Because of Aunt Corrie's influence, tens of thousands of Dutch people were able to forgive Germans for what happened in World War II, and millions of Germans were able to forgive themselves. A single Dutch lady from the tiny nation of Holland influenced millions of people. She impacted nations.

Women Who Impacted the Rise of the Church

The impact of women on the nations is not a new phenomenon. God has used women in powerful ways all through the history of the church. One such woman was Blandina, an apostle and martyr in the early church. She died in 177 AD, during the reign of Emperor Marcus Aurelius. Blandina inspired other believers to face death with courage. It has been said, the martyrdom of Blandina "was not a happy occasion, but it was a victorious one."[3]

The story of Blandina is made known through the writings of Eusebius. In 325 AD, he produced his book, *Ecclesiastical History.* Eusebius writes of Blandina and her courageous leadership of believers being tortured in a Roman amphitheater:

> While we were all afraid . . . Blandina was filled with such power that she was released and rescued from those who took turns torturing her in every way from morning until evening. . . . They marveled that she still remained alive. . . . By her continuous prayer she gave great zeal to the combatants. . . [4]

Blandina was not an exception. Many women were instrumental in the rise of the early church, including Proba and Marcella in the fourth century; Paula, of Roman aristocracy, who developed a women's monastery in Palestine; and Monica, Augustine's mother, who was influential at every turn of the famous writer's life.

Of course, we have not yet spoken of those recorded in Scripture: Phoebe, Chloe, Priscilla, Mary, Martha, Lydia, and the prophesying daughters of Phillip, to name a few. Women sponsored Jesus' ministry,[5] were called disciples,[6] and were present on the day of Pentecost.[7] They led house churches in Philippi and Rome,[8] taught emerging apostles,[9] and prophesied in leadership gatherings.[10]

We cannot deny the impact of great women who were leaders of the early church. And who would want to? They played important roles in the growth of the church and their example inspires us.

Women Reformers

We know about Calvin and Luther, but have you read the amazing story of Katherine Bora Luther, wife of Martin Luther? Luther acknowledged her role in the Reformation when he wrote to her in these telling words, calling her the "...preacher, brewer, gardener, and all things else."[11]

And what of Katherine Zell, known as one of the most outspoken women of the Reformation? She compiled and published hymns, visited those who were sick and in prison, and defended her ministry with these stirring words:

> . . . I have visited the plague-infested and carried out the dead. . . . I have visited those in prison. . . . I have never mounted the pulpit, but I have done more than any minister in visiting those in misery. . . . [12]

Another noteworthy reformer is Argula von Grumback Stauffer, a learned noble lady who challenged university professors to theological debates, offering to base her presentation on nothing other than the Bible. In 1523, she was allowed to present her position before the Holy Roman Empire in Nuremberg. Martin Luther recognized her efforts at reforming the faith, writing:

> The Duke of Bavaria rages above measure, killing, crushing and persecuting the Gospel with all his might. That most noble woman, Argula von Stauffer, is there making a valiant fight with great spirit, boldness of speech, and knowledge of Christ. She deserves that all pray for Christ's victory in her. . . . She alone, among these monsters, carries on with firm faith, though, she admits, not without inner trembling. She is a singular instrument of Christ.[13]

There are many more stories of great women reformers; these are but a few examples. One thing is certain: the silence of Christian history books and commentaries about the role of women reformers is testimony to the bias of the church—to our great shame and loss.

Women Revivalists, Evangelists and Prophetesses

Teacher/evangelist Catherine Booth, co-founder of the Salvation Army, is one of my heroes; as is Susanna Wesley, known as the Mother of Methodism. And I cannot leave out Margaret Fell, early convert and wife of George Fox, founder of the Quakers. Margaret wrote extensively, not only setting out the biblical basis of the Quaker faith, but also defending the rights of women to preach and teach. She was a defender of the movement in the early years, and her doctrinal positions became an integral part of Quaker belief.

Moving forward in church history, we encounter Katherine Kuhlman, who made her mark for God by praying for the sick in healing campaigns. And more currently, Ann Graham Lotz, daughter of Billy Graham, has filled arenas as she teaches God's Word.

According to William H. Cooper, Jr., author of *The Great Revivalists in American Religion, 1740-1944,* another female evangelist, Aimee Semple McPherson, had a "great impact on Pentecostalism, as well as helping bring it out of the theological wilderness and into the acceptable realm of modern Evangelicalism."[14] She built her message and ministry on Hebrews 13:8, "Jesus Christ is the same yesterday, today, and forever." Aimee acted with the same Holy Spirit power as the early church apostles—the power that led them to stand up to Rome, oppose Jewish legalists, and endure great persecution for their faith. Her simple but biblical faith and assurance that God was pouring out his Spirit on all flesh in fulfillment of the prophesy in Joel 2, upended modern Pentecostalism and landed it on its feet—and it landed running, shouting, and praising God!

The list of women God used goes on:

- Jarena Lee – the first widely traveled preacher in the African Methodist Episcopal Church

- Clarissa Danforth – Freewill Baptist revival preacher who saw mighty moves of God in early nineteenth century New England

- Eliza Shirley – launched a series of evangelistic meetings in Philadelphia under the auspices of the Salvation Army, and saw thousands come to Christ

- Amanda Smith – Nineteenth century Negro Holiness preacher and evangelist

- Antoinette Brown – came to Christ through Charles Finney's ministry, and went on to become the first ordained female minister and pastor in America

Women Church Planters and Social Reformers:
From Jungle Pioneers to Urban Servants of the Poor

Women have led the advance of the Gospel through cross-border missions in many countries. "Where are the men?" is the cry of many a mission organization. Why? Because the women have done so poorly? No, because of the absence of men!

J. Hudson Taylor made it clear from the outset: the China Inland Mission would be open to husbands and wives serving side by side in the cause of Christ. He wrote:

It is most important that married missionaries should be double missionaries… unless you intend your wife to be a true missionary, not merely a wife, home-maker and friend, do not join us.[15]

Ann Judson was a jungle pioneer. She and her husband, Adoniram Judson served side by side to reach the Burmese people with the Gospel, and get the Bible translated into their language. After 13 years in Burma, Ann died, still devoted to Jesus. Though she assisted in the translation work, perhaps her greatest contribution was her own inspirational writing. Hampered by health issues and childbearing, she found an outlet in writing to friends and colleagues in Boston. She pleaded her husband's case when he was confined to a death camp for two years. She also wrote eloquently on behalf of the Burmese people, particularly the oppressed Burmese women.

There are so many others we could name; the list of unsung female heroes of faith is long. God alone has recorded their impact on the nations in the journals of heaven. Not a few of them gave up marriage and family for the sake of the Gospel. I honor these amazing women and thank God for them. Whatever your view of women in leadership, please join me in thanking God for the huge sacrifices women have made through the centuries to make Christ known in the nations.

Discussion Questions

1. What stories do you know of women whom God is using in other nations?

2. Why do we not hear more stories of God using women here in the West?

3. The challenge of this chapter is: Why not here? Why not now? Discuss.

4. In light of everything God is doing with women around the world, could anything in your life change?

Chapter 1 Notes

1. Floyd McClung is a highly acclaimed author of many books, including: *Living on the Devil's Doorstep* (Edmunds: YWAM Publishing, 1999), *The Father Heart of God* (Eugene: Harvest House Publishers, 2004), *Follow* (Colorado Springs: David C. Cook, 2010), and *You See Bones, I See an Army* (Edmunds: YWAM Publishing, 2008).

2. Loren Cunningham and David Joel Hamilton, *Why Not Women?* (Seattle: YWAM Publishing, 2000), 67.

3. Ruth A. Tucker and Walter L. Liefeld, *Daughters of the Church,* (Grand Rapids: Zondervan, 1987), 93.

4. Ibid., 94. Quoting from Eusebius, *Ecclesiastical History, V1.*

5. Luke 8:3.

6. For example, Dorcas, Acts 9:36 (NASB).

7. Acts 1:14.

8. Acts 17; Romans 16.

9. Priscilla, Acts 18.

10. Acts 21:9.

11. Tucker and Liefeld, *Daughters of the Church,* 181.

12. Ibid., 184.

13. Ibid., 186.

14. William H. Cooper Jr., *The Great Revivalists in American Religion, 1740-1944: The Careers and Theology of Jonathan Edwards, Charles Finney, Dwight Moody, Billy Sunday and Aimee Semple McPherson,* (Jefferson: McFarland, 2010), 156.

15. Tucker and Liefeld, *Daughters of the Church,* 295. Quoting from J. Hudson Taylor, *God's Man in China,* (Chicago: Moody Press, 1978), 208.

JO SAXTON was born into a Nigerian family and raised in inner city London. She turned down acceptance to the prestigious Oxford University when God called her to give her life to something else, telling her clearly, "Go to Sheffield," a city in South Yorkshire, England. A college student there, she joined St. Thomas' Church, just as leader Mike Breen was launching what are now known as missional communities (a group of people, about the size of an extended family, on mission together). This movement focuses churches on neighborhoods and networks for the purpose of Gospel-centered city transformation. Jo volunteered at St. Thomas' throughout her college years, later became the church's youth pastor, and then the college ministry pastor. During this time, she also planted a missional community. When Mike moved on from St. Thomas' in 2004, he gathered a team to work with him at a church in the US. Jo and her husband, Chris, were part of this team, and 3DM was born. Jo is a leader within the 3DM movement— training female leaders, developing training for young adults, and working with church leaders and teams on living missionally in an increasingly post-Christian context. Today, Jo and Chris are both pastors and have two daughters. Jo also serves as the equipping director at a Lutheran Church in Minneapolis, training leaders across all departments of the church. She is author of *More Than Enchanting: Breaking Through Barriers to Influence Your World,* which encourages women to use their God-given talents and embrace the calling to seek his Kingdom above all else.

CHAPTER 2
MISSION CRITICAL

By Dave Ferguson

Do women play a vital role in accomplishing the mission of Jesus here on earth? Dave Ferguson thinks so. He believes the workforce for the harvest will increase exponentially when women are encouraged to co-labor alongside men.

When we first heard how Dave and his church came to the conclusion that women are welcomed into every aspect of church life, we knew it was a story worth telling. But Dave not only empowers the women in his own church, he also has a personal story to tell.

Dave is an author, a speaker, and one of the co-founders of Exponential—a community of leaders committed to multiplying healthy, reproducing faith communities. They run the annual Exponential conference for church planters. He is a lead pastor and spiritual entrepreneur with Community Christian Church and the NewThing network.

Community Christian Church was a brand new church and, as the church planter, I appointed a group of people who would serve as our Leadership Advisory Team. This team of men and women was responsible to hold me (and my young staff of 20-year-olds) accountable, as well as establish our first group of elders.

For two years, we met, prayed, studied, and discussed the role of women in leadership. We found the Bible was very clear about the role and expectation of an elder on a number of issues, but lacked clarity regarding gender. Was the role of elder just for men? Or was service in this oversight role based on the gifting of the individual man or woman?

Two Years of Not Hurrying

During the next 24 months, I reasoned with some of the greatest theological minds, best leaders, and most God-honoring people I have ever known, about the role of women in church leadership. Since this book is advocating for women leaders, you might think we quickly concluded that women could serve as leaders and elders. However, that was not the case. In fact, during those two years, every person on that exceptional team found themselves swaying back and forth on this controversial issue. Why did we take so long to discern what Scripture has to say? Let me give you a few reasons, and in the process, encourage you to "not be hasty in the laying on of hands"[1] but give serious thought and time to this issue.

- **It takes time to set aside your assumptions and open yourself up to solid theological reasoning.** None of our team members had ever been a part of a church that allowed women to serve as elders, so we assumed this was a male-only role—until we examined some Scripture that seemed to suggest otherwise. It would have been quick and easy for us to stick with our assumptions. Instead, we took the time to put our understood notions aside and open our hearts to what the Bible actually had to say.

- **It takes time to make a good decision, especially when the subject is controversial.** There were two groups of people in our church— one way or the other, this would be an unpopular decision. Our church primarily consisted of previously unchurched people who didn't live in the Bible Belt and assumed women could serve in any role. But we also had a small group of leaders from an Independent Christian Church background, the kind of church I grew up in, and they assumed women could not serve as elders. We took our time because we knew this decision would not be easily embraced or immediately welcomed by one of the groups.

- **It takes time to get the decision right.** Rather than put pressure on ourselves to come to a conclusion within a certain time frame, we suspended any deadline and focused on making a good and godly decision. As author Peter Drucker said, "Good decisions are not so much made as they become apparent." We didn't force this decision, but a good and right decision became apparent over time.

If you find yourself in a church leadership position and are wrestling with a decision about the role of women in the church, for these reasons and more, I would encourage you to take your time.

And the Decision of the Jury...

After two years, the Leadership Advisory Team came to a decision. The following is an excerpt from an appendix to our constitution and bylaws:

> The Leadership Advisory Team (LAT) spent two years formulating the Constitution and bylaws of Community Christian Church. The process included diligent study, prayer, reflection, consultation, and discussion. We believe the Bible teaches (and the leadership history of our church supports) that men and women are full partners in ministry in the kingdom of God. Giftedness by the Holy Spirit is the primary basis of qualification for ministry (Romans 12:1-8; I Corinthians 12 & 14; Ephesians 4:1-16; I Peter 4:10-11). We do not find the whole witness and testimony of Scripture sufficiently consistent with the position of male-only governance.
>
> We believe our position is consistent with the following Scriptures:
>
> Women in the New Testament church were leaders serving as prophets (Acts 21:9), teachers (Acts 18:26), ministers (Romans 16:1-3), leaders in worship services (I Corinthians 11:4-5) and co-workers with the Apostle Paul (Philippians 4:2-3).
>
> The Holy Spirit empowers both men and women, young and old to speak for God (Acts 2:17-18).

Men and women are equal recipients of God's gifts (I Peter 3:7).

In Christ all people, male and female, are to be submissive to one another and to serve one another in reciprocal love and obedience to Jesus (Ephesians 5:21; Philippians 2:3-4; Galatians 5:13).

In the Old Testament a woman was appointed by God to be the principal leader of the nation of Israel (Judges 4-5).

We believe these passages suggest that no person be disqualified from any form of service in the body of Christ based solely on gender.

Once we came to our conclusion, we put together a process to communicate this decision to our leaders and church members. While the process was solid, as anticipated, the decision was not well-received by some. We had several people and families who grew up in male-only-led churches; they were sure we had abandoned Scripture for cultural acceptance and were now headed down the slippery slope toward heresy. These were people I really loved, and I believe they loved me, but ultimately they left our church. It was the hardest time in the life of our church.

This was a decision we came to almost 20 years ago. With the perspective that time brings, I can say with confidence what did and did not motivate this decision:

- **Our decision was not based on being egalitarian.** Community Christian is a church founded with the mission of "helping people find their way back to God," and has no theological investment in equality, in the modern sense of the way the word is used politically. Our decision was not about an equal rights orientation.

- **Our decision was not informed by feminism.** While we believe that feminism as a contemporary movement has made both positive and negative contributions, Community Christian has no particular alignment with a feminist perspective on this issue or any other.

- **Our decision was based on the whole testimony of Scripture.** We concluded the Bible clearly shows that women led at all levels in the first century church, including as an apostle (Junia).[2] We also concluded any scriptural injunctions that seemed to forbid female leadership did not hold up to exegetical scrutiny of the whole witness and testimony of Scripture: women prophesied, women taught, women were apostles. While there are not any female elders named in Scripture, we also have no names of male elders. If someone wants to make an argument from silence and say, "Name one female elder in the Bible," you can't. But you can't name a male elder either.

- **Our decision was based on how the Holy Spirit gifts people to lead.** This decision was made by taking the less-restrictive view and focusing on how the Spirit gifts people individually. If someone is gifted to serve and lead in any capacity, we found nothing in Scripture to suggest their gender should qualify or disqualify them.

A Changed Mind:
Theologically Right, but not Critical for the Mission

It wasn't long before word began to get out to other churches and church leaders, "Community has women elders!" For some groups, that meant we were heretics—we'd become their next whipping post and an example of a church that doesn't take Scripture seriously. But other churches and church leaders were curious and wanted to hear more about how we arrived at such a position.

I remember getting a call from a prominent church leader, asking me to speak to a group about women, leadership, and our position on this issue in the church. As I considered the request, I also reflected on the two-year journey with our Leadership Advisory Team. I had reached a decision along with a team of respected, thoughtful, godly leaders, and felt certain we were theologically right, but I also believed this issue was not mission critical. I can remember responding to the speaking request with this answer: "No, this is not the hill I want to die on. When people remember me, I want to die on the hill of helping people find their way back to God—not the issue of women in leadership." And I felt content with that answer for the next 10 years.

A Changed Heart: Theologically Right *and* Mission Critical

My feelings about the issue of women in leadership began to change when my oldest child, Amy, started looking for colleges. Like many 18-years-olds, she wasn't sure what she wanted to declare as a major, but student ministry was toward the top of her list of interests. So with ministry as a strong consideration, we began looking for a Christian college that would be a good fit.

I had two criteria in mind as we began our search: first, I wanted her to find a school with a strong commitment to the authority of Scripture, and second, I wanted her to attend a school that would encourage her as a female leader to fulfill her God-given potential. As we began our search locally, then expanded nationally, we discovered you could have one or the other, but seldom both. You could either attend a school that believed and taught the authority of Scripture, but had few, if any, female women on their practical ministry staff. Or, they had many women on staff and a culture that encouraged female leaders, but were not consistently strong about biblical authority.

With each college visit, there was a growing realization that finding a school where my daughter could get a solid theological education along with positive encouragement to use all of her gifts was going to be very hard. That's when it got personal and something began to change in me. The issue of women in leadership went from being something that was theologically right, but not mission critical, to both theologically correct *and* critical for accomplishing the mission of Jesus!

It was like my eyes were opened—for the first time, I realized that 50 percent of the leaders God had gifted for this mission were not mobilized or utilized. I don't know how I missed it before. It was like the church was trying to show off by doing everything with one hand tied behind her back! The more I thought about it, the more ridiculous it seemed. I began to look at the world through the eyes of my daughter (and other women) and saw very limited possibilities for her to use her gifts. It was suddenly personal and emotional.

Strategy for Mobilizing the Other Fifty Percent

After experiencing a change of mind, and then a change of heart, I knew this issue was not detached from the mission of Jesus. This was not an issue I could set aside as less than mission critical. If the dream of the Gospel movement is ever to be realized, we must mobilize every male and female. But how? How can we bring other people and leaders like myself—who already believe women can and should lead, but have been passive—on a journey to see that it is mission critical? We can lead them, one by one, through this process: observation, inspiration, and application. Let me give you an overview, and then explain in more detail.

OBSERVATION: The first move in realizing a new tomorrow is seeing a different today. We have to spark the imagination of the people and leaders in the church by letting them see women functioning in roles of leadership. When they are able to observe women in these roles, the imagination is set free; women and men alike will dream dreams and see new visions.

INSPIRATION: The second move is inspiring the hearts and minds of church people and their leadership. When it becomes emotional and personal, lasting change will occur and the status quo will no longer be acceptable.

APPLICATION: The final move is when churches and their leaders, who were once passive, now see that female leadership is critical to the mission. It is with keen understanding and heartfelt passion that churches and their leadership will begin to intentionally develop and deploy women leaders.

Strategic Step 1: OBSERVATION

The first step on the journey is the ability to see the future—by envisioning women in roles that were once thought only for men, you change the future. We can begin simply: by giving women leaders a place on the platform, by sharing stories, by issuing a rebuke when needed. Bill Gates recalls once being invited to speak in Saudi Arabia and finding himself facing a segregated audience. Four-fifths of the listeners were men, on the left. The remaining one-fifth was women—covered by black cloaks and veils—on the right. A partition separated the two groups. During the question-and-answer session, a member of the audience noted that Saudi Arabia aimed to be one of the top 10 countries in the world in technology by 2010 and asked if that was realistic.

"Well, if you're not fully utilizing half the talent in the country," Gates said, "you're not going to get too close to the top ten."

I wonder if God doesn't hear our prayers for revival and movement and say, "You are already gifted and ready for revival and movement—if you would only utilize more than half the talent I gave you."

One of my favorite stories regarding women of influence is about Tammy Melchien. Four years ago, Tammy began to sense God calling her to plant a campus of Community Christian Church in the city of Chicago. Up to that point, we had not been successful in planting campuses in the city; all our locations were in the suburbs. We needed just the right leader to launch this important new site.

Tammy is a very bright woman whom God had continually put into positions of influence. She had received encouragement to use her gifts and proven successful in leading ministries, both inside and outside the local church. Like many on our staff, Tammy raised her own salary and proved she could start something from nothing. In every role we gave her, she not only excelled personally, but also did an outstanding job of developing other leaders around her.

We agreed that Tammy was the right leader to start a new campus in the Lincoln Square neighborhood of Chicago. My brother, Jon, who would oversee Tammy, also saw this as an opportunity to influence other church leaders to give women executive leadership opportunities. Since then, Tammy has done a great job launching this new site, building relationships with the local school and neighbors, teaching/preaching on weekends, and continuing to develop leaders around her. Our dream is to one day see 200 locations of Community in the city and suburbs of Chicago. I believe God used Tammy to give that dream a real possibility by establishing our first site in the city.

I love telling Tammy's story of starting a church from scratch because it allows other women with the gift of leadership to see what they too can do! Her story illustrates the first step on this journey—

seeing, and helping others see, what women can and should do for the Kingdom. Ask yourself: What female leader can I platform? Do I need to speak the truth when women are so obviously vacant from leadership roles? What stories of influential women can I tell? Observation is where it all begins.

Strategic Step 2: INSPIRATION

If the first step on the journey is with the eyes, the second step is one of heart and mind. My friend Alan Hirsch, co-author of *On the Verge* and co-contributor to *The Black Swan Effect,* was recently speaking at a conference when he said, "The church has all too often treated women like the Taliban has treated them—only perhaps more subtly. Clearly we do not condone the crude and explicit violence they inflict on women, but we hardly treat them any better when it comes to their equal dignity, status, and function in Christ." While he was speaking, you could almost feel people's minds churning and thinking. We have to shake-up people intellectually and help them see the current practices of many churches for what they really are.

Another friend and partner in church planting, Greg Nettle, also spoke on women in the church. He pointed out some important observations from Scripture:

- **Men and women are both created in the image of God and are therefore of equal value before God.** Genesis 1:27-28 tells us, "So God created human beings in his own image. In the image of God he created them; male and female he created them. Then God blessed them and said, 'Be fruitful and multiply. Fill the earth and govern it. Reign over the fish in the sea, the birds in the sky, and all the animals that scurry along the ground.'" Women and men, both created in God's image, are of equal value and were given equal authority and responsibility. That was God's intent from the beginning.

- **Men and women are both uniquely gifted by God and should be given opportunities for the full expression of their giftedness.** Ephesians 4:7 (NLT) reminds us that God "has given each one of us a special gift through the generosity of Christ." Notice that it does not say God "has given every *man* a special gift." If we skip down to verse 11 it says, "Now these are the gifts Christ gave to the church: the apostles, the prophets, the evangelists, and the pastors and teachers." So, we have these gifts that are given to each one of us, both men and women. Who gives the gifts? God gives the gifts. He determines every man's and every woman's unique gifting. Our job is simply to use our gifts and help others in the body of Christ fully use theirs as well.

- **Both men and women are given gifts to serve others.** First Corinthians 12:7 tells us, "A spiritual gift is given to each of us so we can help each other." We need every man and woman to discover their spiritual gifts so that the church can function to its full capacity.

Doesn't this make you rethink gifts, service, and how God equips the church? A recent *Harvard Business Review* article titled, "Are Women Better Leaders Than Men?,"[4] highlights what the church is missing by not having more women leaders. The article was based on extensive research, in which individuals were asked to rate a leader's overall effectiveness and judge their strength in 16 areas of competency (shown by 30 years of research to be important factors in leadership effectiveness). Leaders were rated by their peers, bosses, direct reports, and other associates on criteria such as: taking the initiative, developing others, inspiring and motivating, and pursuing their own development. The results? At every level, women rated better as overall leaders than their male counterparts—and the higher the level, the wider the gap.

Overall Leadership Effectiveness by Gender, by Position (Percentile Scores)		
Position	Male	Female
Top Management, Executive, Senior Team Members	57.7	67.7
Reports to Top Management, Supervises Middle Managers	48.9	56.2
Middle Manager	49.9	52.7
Supervisors, Front Line Manager, Foreman	52.5	52.6
Individual Contributor	52.7	53.9
Other	50.7	52.0
Total	51.3	55.1
Source: Zenger Folkman Inc., 2011		

Don't those results make you ask some questions? Don't you wonder how God could make so many women outstanding leaders in the marketplace, but not want them to lead in the church or ministry? Does it disturb you a little that the results suggest women are actually better at leading than men? We need to constantly inspire people to rethink their position on this issue. Are they comfortable with the status quo? Should women in the church be relegated to working only with children and other women?

Strategic Step 3: APPLICATION

After seeing it with our eyes, then being moved in our hearts and minds, the last step on this journey is with our hands. When we convince churches that releasing all of God's people is critical to the mission, they will put their hands to the plow and develop and deploy every person we have for the mission—both men and women!

In *On The Verge*, we present the biblical case that the way to accomplish the mission of Jesus is through a missional movement. We contend that the church—in its original form, the state in which

God intended it—is a movement. The church was never meant to be merely a place to come on Sundays, or a place to outsource individual spiritual needs. The church was designed to be a movement that accomplishes the Acts 1:8 vision of Jesus—reaching and restoring "Jerusalem…Judea…Samaria…and the ends of the earth."

So what does a movement look like? I believe this simple diagram is a great expression of the church of Jesus as a missional movement:

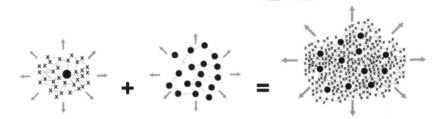

- **Missional People:** First, initiating a movement requires every person to be on mission. This means everyone who claims to be a Christ-follower is "doing the good work that God prepared in advance for him or her to do."[5] We need churches that mobilize every gifted man and every gifted woman for the cause of the mission.

- **Multiplying Churches:** Second, it requires the multiplication of churches. By God's design, the church can have lots of varied and creative expressions, but for there to be movement, those expressions must multiply.

- **Missional Movement:** When you put missional people together with multiplying churches, it works much like the two pedals of a bike. You push the first pedal of missional people, and then you push the second pedal of multiplying churches—as you do, you begin to move forward. With each push on the pedal, you gain more and more momentum. Eventually, you experience movement.

If we refuse to deploy 50 percent of those missional people to their fullest potential, it becomes exponentially more difficult to create movement. At some level, it just becomes plain stupid! We need every man on mission. *And,* we need every woman on mission.

I recently had an experience that reignited in me a desire to "die on the hill" of advocating for women in leadership. I had just finished teaching a workshop on church planting when I met Jayla, a woman I guessed to be in her late 20s. I had already noticed her listening intently to every part of the presentation and I could tell by her follow-up questions that she was well-read and passionate about the topic. As we talked, I learned how she became a Christ-follower, how God consistently put her in places of influence and about her passionate desire to trade her life for the mission of Jesus. I was impressed. As we were walking out of the building, I asked her, "Have you ever thought about planting a church?"

She literally stopped walking. Her eyes opened wide. She shook her head slowly back and forth and told me, "No one has ever asked me that before." Jayla explained this was not a possibility in the churches she had been part of—women didn't lead, and women didn't plant churches.

My conversation with Jayla has been burned into my conscience as a reminder of something that is very wrong! Within the circles I travel, a sharp, young, twentysomething male showing obvious leadership potential would have been asked dozens of times if he had ever considered planting a church. But not her! I walked away from that experience saying to myself, "This has to change! For Jayla it has to change. For the sake of the mission, this has to change."

It truly is mission critical.

Discussion Questions

1. Do you personally believe the role of women is mission critical? Why?

2. Where does your faith community sit on the spectrum Dave discusses in this chapter—are women considered irrelevant or mission critical? Why does your faith community believe the way it does?

3. What difference do you think the full participation of women will make to Jesus' mission to reach the world with the good news?

4. If the role of women was viewed as mission critical, what difference could this make in your life? In your church?

Chapter 2 Notes

1. 1 Timothy 5:22 (NIV).

2. Romans 16:7.

3. According to theologian Philip B. Payne, the Bible gives John (2 John 1 and 3 John 1) and Peter (2 Pet. 5:1) special titles containing the word "elder," but they refer to their special status as apostolic eyewitnesses. They do not identify them as having a local church office.

4. "Are Women Better Leaders than Men?," Jack Zenger and Joseph Folkman, *Harvard Business Review,* March 15, 2012, http://blogs.hbr.org/2012/03 /a-study-in-leadership-women-do/.

5. Ephesians 2:10 (author's own paraphrase).

LINDA HARTZELL grew up in a quiet, conservative, South Dakota ranch town, but by the time she was in high school, she was tough and wayward. Consequently, she spent a lot of time being disciplined in the principal's office. During her junior year of high school, Linda had a dramatic encounter with the Lord that would change the course of her life. Through the vulnerable years of spiritual growth that followed, Linda was discipled and grounded by a handful of diverse, wonderful men and women who poured into her, and gave her time and space to grow. Linda has now lived by faith for more than 30 years. She has made dozens of trips on assignment with the Lord into 48 nations. She is bilingual, an author, holds a doctorate in theology, and serves as an international representative for End Time Handmaidens, a global missionary organization with a focus on prayer, fasting, and prophetic ministry to the nations. At times, she preaches to crowds from 10,000 to 25,000. When asked to respond to the notion that she couldn't be a woman in five-fold ministry, Linda gently replied, "Actually, no one ever told me I couldn't."

CHAPTER 3

WOMEN ON MISSION

By Felicity Dale

If, as Dave Ferguson suggests, the inclusion of women is critical for accomplishing the mission of Jesus, then changing women's mindset regarding their role in the church becomes a matter of urgency.

A question that has puzzled our team of women for some time is this: In situations where there are no theological barriers to overcome and women are encouraged to take the initiative, why do so few step up to the plate? Do they still feel the need to wait for a man to follow? Do they believe it's necessary to have a man's permission to act? Why are they content to sit passively, watching men start Kingdom ventures?

I faced some of these same issues. In the UK, during the 1970s and '80s, the gender debate was still raging, and the stream of churches I belonged to held the opinion that women should not take roles with authority over men. When I moved to the United States and became involved in the simple/organic church movement, I was free to follow the Holy Spirit wherever he led.

Even though I'd been trained as a physician (a male-dominated profession), I was shocked by how natural it was to expect my husband to take the initiative in ministry. But over time, through God's grace and guidance, I found my place and answered my calling as a ministry leader, trainer, church planter, blogger, and author.[1] This is the story of how I broke free.

The temperature was minus 13 degrees. The church hostel where we were staying was unheated because there were so few visitors in January, and despite wearing several layers of clothing, we couldn't get warm. It was 1983. Tony, my husband, and I were in Seoul, South Korea to visit the Yoido Full Gospel Church—the largest church in the world—led by Dr. David Yonggi Cho.

One day, to get warm, we headed over to the church's heated administration building. As we wandered along the hallways between the various offices, someone approached us.

"Would you like an interview with Dr. Cho?"

Much to our surprise, we were ushered into Dr. Cho's office and had a 20-minute conversation with him. He shared much with us about the nature of revival and the crucial importance of prayer, but the thing that has most stood out over the years is this: "You in the West will never see a move of God until you use your women."

Prayer was one key to this extraordinary growth in Korea, but women have also played a vital role. In 1958, Yoido Full Gospel Church saw its humble beginnings in the home of Choi Ja-shil (who later became Dr. Cho's mother-in-law). As the church grew, Dr. Cho took on more and more responsibilities until he became exhausted and ill. At this point, God challenged him to release women. The church now numbers more than 800,000.[2] Two-thirds of the associate pastors are women, and 47,000 of the 50,000 cell group leaders are women too.

Three decades have passed since our conversation with Dr. Cho, and what he predicted for us has sadly proven true. The church in the West has not used its women, nor—with one or two possible exceptions—have we seen any major, long-lasting, and wide-sweeping revivals. Whereas Korea has grown from a 2 percent Christian population in 1945 to about 30 percent today, we in the West have gone backwards. In the UK, where I am from, Christianity is irrelevant to the vast majority of the population. Here in the United States, we may be only a generation away from being a post-Christian nation.

Korea is not the only success story. Women have been key to seeing a great harvest in other nations too. Even in countries that are traditionally hostile to the Gospel, women are fearlessly going into dangerous situations and spreading the good news, making disciples, and starting churches.

According to Jesus, if there's a lack of harvest, it's not because the harvest is especially difficult, it's due to a lack of workers.[3] His solution? Pray for workers. This not only includes existing Christians, but also those who don't yet know the Lord—not only men, but also women. Unfortunately, the church often sidelines many of its available workers for the harvest; most notably, women. Their part in engaging new disciples is typically limited to inviting friends to attend church with them. If we truly want to see a great harvest, women will take on roles traditionally assigned to men. They need to make disciples and baptize them, to teach and train, to start churches, to give Communion, to strategize for the harvest.

If women are one of the keys to a greater harvest, then we need to rethink their status. If the inclusion of women in strategic roles is going to make a difference in the size and quality of the harvest, then it's vital to liberate them into their full potential.

The revival in Korea has lasted for decades. Fully involving women has been key to other long-lasting revivals as well. Women led Wesley's class meetings, and he even recommended them to preach.[4] When Wesley was asked why he encouraged certain females to preach, he replied, "Because God owns them in the conversion of sinners, and who am I that I should withstand God?"[5] Another example, the Moravians, selected women to serve as elders alongside the men. In China, women still account for more than 80 percent of house church leaders and itinerant evangelists.

Why is it important that women break free from their constraints? When women co-labor alongside men in the Kingdom, the workforce for the harvest is potentially doubled. The effect is synergistic. As more and more women move out into their God-given destiny, they blaze a trail for other women to follow.

But it's not always easy for those of us who were brought up in a patriarchal system.

Lessons from Our Chocolate Lab

Tony and I used to have a dog called Sugar—a faithful and loyal companion, though of dubious parentage and limited intelligence. Sugar had one major character flaw. She loved to wander. We live in a house with a fenced yard and an electric gate across the driveway. Sugar used to hide, lying in wait, until a car went through the gate. Then, just as the gate was closing the final few inches, she would make her bid for freedom. She would return several hours later, exhausted but happy.

When we decided to put a stop to her adventures, we installed an invisible fence across the driveway. If dogs approach an invisible fence too closely, a little battery on their collar gives them a small jolt of electricity. They soon learn their boundaries.

After a couple of, shall we say, shocking experiences, Sugar learned to stay within the confines of our yard. In fact, long after the battery in her collar had died, Sugar would sit, wistfully gazing at the liberty that lay on the other side of an open gate without making any attempt to escape. She had become conditioned to her limitations.

As women in the church, we too, have been conditioned to live within boundaries.

The Hemiplegic Bride

Hemiplegia is a medical term used to describe paralysis on one side of the body that occurs, for example, after a stroke. In the same way, the body of Christ in the West could be described as hemiplegic. The female half of the body of Christ is, for the most part, weak—not functioning well because women have been left out of strategic roles.

Let me illustrate the kind of problem women sometimes face.

One Saturday morning a few years ago, Tony and I were enjoying a lie-in when his cell phone rang. The person at the other end was discussing publishing a book I had written, so naturally, I was interested in the conversation. I mouthed to Tony, "Put it on speaker phone."

The conversation continued. After a while, the man said, "Of course, we'll have both your names on the front cover. This book is far too important to have been written by a woman!"

Upon hearing this, I suffered a temporary loss of sanctification. In that one sentence, the person had epitomized the problem that exists for many women in the church, one that had caused me much confusion and angst throughout the years.

Traditional Christian Culture for Women

I was born again into a Christian culture that dictated men lead, women follow. For various "scriptural reasons," women were to be quiet, submissive followers. They were only allowed to minister in certain ways: they could teach a Sunday school class, lead a prayer ministry, or run a vacation Bible school. And let's not forget the premiere women's ministry, they could make coffee. (Actually, making coffee is a task specifically designated for men. There's an entire book of the Bible dedicated to it—the Book of He Brews!) But a woman teaching on Sunday morning? No way! A woman baptizing? Perish the thought! Or a woman in a position of strategic overall leadership? Impossible!

I know this isn't true right across the denominational spectrum. I praise God for denominations, such as Foursquare, who pioneered the advancement of women in ministry. But the British House Church Movement we were part of in earlier days believed very strongly that only men could lead. Tony used to attend frequent men's leadership weekends, while I was left behind to look after our four children. He would return full of glowing reports of how God had moved in incredible power. Don't get me wrong—I was glad Tony was blessed, and I loved being with my kids. I just found it very difficult to be excluded from where the Lord seemed to be moving most strongly—in the men-only gatherings. (Thankfully, that particular stream of churches has totally changed its stance on women and now champions their right and ability to move in any way God chooses.)

For me, the prohibitions because of my gender caused much heartache for many years. I've always had a longing and gifting to hear from God and think strategically, and it was extremely difficult for me to be excluded from decision-making purely because I'm not male. I frequently asked the Lord why he had given me these gifts and desire if I couldn't use them for his glory.

Helpmates and Heroines

In the church, I was given the impression that a woman's role was to be that of a "helpmeet" for her husband—some kind of divinely appointed personal assistant. Partly, this was the influence of traditional secular society that, for centuries, assigned women (unless they were poor) one of two roles:

1. Women are mere reflections of their husbands, uninterested in "important" things like finance, politics, or religion. They enhance their husband's reputations by looking pretty and acting according to convention. They spend their time in fripperies and trivia.

2. Women's place is at home. They should run a good household, bring up their children well, and engage in wholesome social activities. Their concerns are wrapped up in the household.

In either case, women's opinions were considered uninformed and unimportant. Thankfully, society is changing. But is the church?

The church in which I learned most of my basic doctrines reinforced the irrelevance of women. Even though no one explicitly stated it, the obvious conclusion was that God, for some divine reason, prefers men. Women are therefore inferior to men, comparatively unimportant in the bigger scheme of life in the Kingdom. And a whole generation of women has been brought up to believe this was true. I was told:

- Of course I can lead—but only through my influence on my husband.

- Women are equal to men. It's just that their roles are different. (This is a Christian version of the statement in *Animal Farm,* by George Orwell:[6] "All animals are equal, but some animals are more equal than others.")

- I am always to submit to a man's authority. If I'm unmarried or my husband is not around, I have to find a man to "cover" me.

- I can never hold any position of strategic influence or leadership in the church.

- I need a man's permission before I do anything in the Kingdom.

- My husband is the leader; I am there to serve his calling and vision. His destiny counts more than mine.

- I cannot teach a man under any circumstances.

- Because Eve was deceived, as a woman, I am more open to deception than a man, and likely to lead the church astray.

- God created Adam before he created Eve. Therefore, men lead; women follow.

- A strong woman probably has a "Jezebel spirit."

- God using a woman is an exception—like when he spoke through Balaam's ass.

- Once I have children, my place is in the home.

- There are plenty of ministries I can be involved in—prayer and women's ministries, Sunday school, etc. I should be content with this, and not seek to use my gifting outside of those boundaries.

- The only time a woman can lead is when God cannot find a man to do the job.

This last one legitimized women on the mission field. Many of them were my heroines. I devoured their biographies as a young believer. I remember reading about Amy Carmichael of Dohnavaur, India. She founded a mission and an orphanage, serving in India for 55 years without a furlough. Her writings were very inspiring. I was also challenged by the story of Gladys Aylwood, the "little woman," who began as a domestic worker in London, but was determined to go to China as a missionary. Turned down by mission societies because of her lack of education, she spent her life savings to purchase a one-way ticket. For a time, she worked as a "foot inspector," traveling around China's countryside to enforce laws against binding women's feet. When the Japanese invaded in 1938, she led 94 orphans over the mountains to safety. She eventually moved to Taiwan, where she became a friend of Tony's family, living with them for several months.

I have the privilege of knowing several other heroines of the faith—women who are household names in the Christian world. Jackie Pullinger is a family friend. She worked in the Walled City—a part of Hong Kong that, until the government demolished it, was renowned for lawlessness, crime and Triad activity. Jackie rescues drug addicts from the street, taking them to a place of safety to recover from their addictions. She founded the St. Stephen's Society that now provides a home for more than 200 recovering addicts.

Heidi Baker works with her husband, Rolland, in Mozambique. (Rolland and Tony went to the same school for missionary kids in Taiwan.) They rescue orphans from the streets and garbage dumps, bringing them to live at their centers—feeding, clothing, and educating them. The couple preaches in the villages, seeing thousands find the Lord. More than 10,000 churches have started under their ministry in Mozambique and in the surrounding nations.

These women are outstanding leaders in their own right, in their various spheres of ministry. God finds no contradiction in using women in extraordinary ways.

I was bewildered by the role of women in the West. If women can move under the Holy Spirit's leading in cross-cultural missions, I reasoned, why can't the Lord use women in the West in similar ways? As a physician, I was making life and death decisions for my patients, but because of my gender, I wasn't allowed to be strategic within the church. I was hurt and baffled by this, but finally came to accept that if this is the way God wanted it, I would learn to live within the limitations imposed by a patriarchal system.

Freedom at Last

In 1987, we moved from England to the States. After nine years of God's school on the backside of the desert, we became involved in the simple/organic church movement. I soon discovered there are no barriers for women within this movement—Tony and I are both encouraged and equipped to do anything the Lord calls us to. There is complete freedom for us to function as God intends.

I have women friends who move powerfully in the five-fold ministry gifts described in Ephesians 4. Some are apostles in their regions. They gather people together strategically, organizing conferences or traveling to encourage those who are just starting on the church planting journey. Several are involved not only in starting churches, but also in training others to do the same. Other women move powerfully in the gift of prophecy, speaking strategically from God into different situations. I have a friend who leads people to the Lord wherever she goes. She is a remarkable evangelist. Many women have a pastoral heart; some are gifted teachers.

But these examples are the minority. For the most part, women tend to stay within the roles they learned in traditional church. Why? For some, it's an easy excuse for laziness or fear. But for others, like Sugar with her collar, even though they now have freedom, they have become conditioned to stay within their boundaries.

The Example of Slavery

One of the most helpful parallels I've found is that of slavery. Those who opposed the abolition of slavery used the Bible to support their contention that slavery was God's will for mankind. There were five main points to their argument:[7]

1. God established slavery.

2. Slavery was practiced in the Old Testament by righteous people like Abraham.

3. The moral law sanctioned and regulated slavery.

4. Jesus accepted slavery. (The word, *doulos* or slave is found more than 70 times in the Gospels.)

5. The apostles upheld slavery.

If God endorses slavery in the Bible, why don't Christians today fight for its reinstatement? We all instinctively know that Jesus came to loose the chains of captivity in whatever form they are found.

It was Christians who were primarily responsible for the abolition of slavery. They found plenty of evidence in the Bible to support the argument against slavery. The movie, *Amazing Grace*, reveals the important role William Wilberforce had in the cessation of slavery in the British Empire. Harriet Beecher Stowe, author of *Uncle Tom's Cabin*, an anti-slavery novel, was very influential in the United States through her writings. Both were passionate Christians. They knew that abolition lines up with the Bible's clear, overall teaching about freedom—by Jesus and the other New Testament writers, and in the Old Testament as well (God made specific arrangements for slaves to be released).

But the parallel of slavery extends further. Harriet Tubman, who led many slaves to freedom through the Underground Railroad, said, "I freed a thousand slaves. I would've freed a thousand more if only they knew they were slaves."

After the Emancipation, most slaves stayed where they were. Some had no idea they were now free, and others had no idea how to survive outside of slavery. Many entered into sharecropping arrangements with their former masters, getting paid a pittance for the same work they had formerly done as slaves. It took generations for the reality of freedom to take effect.

The worst kind of prison is that of the mind, where a person accepts adverse circumstances as the natural order of things without realizing the perceived cage bars don't really exist. They are held captive only by their own thoughts. As women, many of us are imprisoned by what we have known from the past.

Understanding the Challenging Scriptures

For me, the path to freedom was not quick and easy. The first and most important step was to seek fresh understanding of Scriptures that had shaped my thinking on this issue in the past, such as

1 Corinthians 14 and 1 Timothy 2. They can be understood with integrity to mean something other than what I had always been taught. The whole trend and tenor of the Scriptures is toward liberty.

With this in mind, let's look at 1 Corinthians 14:34-35:

> Women should be silent during the church meetings. It is not proper for them to speak. They should be submissive, just as the law says. If they have any questions, they should ask their husbands at home, for it is improper for women to speak in church meetings.

As I studied this Scripture, I realized there are two other sets of people who were told to keep silent (Greek word, *sigao)* in this chapter—those speaking in tongues when there was no interpreter present[8] and those prophesying when another person received a word of prophecy.[9]

The context of these verses is important to consider. The Apostle Paul is answering questions posed to him in a letter from the Corinthians.[10] You can picture the letter: "Paul, what should we do when someone speaks in tongues and there is no one to interpret?" Paul repeats the question and then gives his answer. The same is true with the question about how to handle prophesying. No one assumed that Paul's answer meant their silence was to be ongoing and in every circumstance. The problem with the verse about women keeping silent is that we don't know the question. When I understood this, I realized the silence of women was only for the particular situation described in Corinth at that time.

Another Scripture interpretation that gave me freedom came in the translation of the word "helper" from Genesis 2, verses 18 and 20. None of the animals God created was a "helper fit" for Adam, and so the Lord fashioned woman from Adam's side. Whereas in the past, I had assumed from this that a wife was supposed to help her husband fulfill the vision God has given him, I was astounded to discover how the word "helper" (Hebrew word, *ezer)* is typically used throughout Scripture. Of the 21 times it is used in the Old Testament, all but five instances use *ezer* in reference to God, sometimes in a decidedly militaristic context.

Here's an example of how *ezer* is used in Psalm 121:1-2 (NKJV):

> I will lift up my eyes to the hills—from whence comes my help *(ezer)*? My help *(ezer)* comes from the Lord, who made heaven and earth.

Far from being a divine assistant, her husband's personal Girl Friday, a wife is to be more of a consultant, a coach, a rescuer—an equal, walking alongside with wisdom to impart.

Healing

That freed me from a scriptural point of view, but there were other barriers to face on a personal level. Was I worthy? Years of assuming my contributions were less valuable made me wonder. Were men simply better-suited for some roles than women?

I am totally blessed to be married to a wonderful husband. Tony is a gifted communicator who thinks on his feet and expresses himself eloquently. My speaking was a comparative disaster. Surely, I reasoned, it's better to let others hear Tony rather than me. But as Tony laid down his role as primary communicator—refusing to take the major role of speaking from the platform and asking me to share alongside him—I gained confidence, and began to see how the Lord could use me as a public speaker.

Although I had come a long way, I often continued to feel subconsciously guilty that I was usurping a man's authority. (I knew this has not been a deliberate misogyny in most cases—the guys have simply been trying to follow the Scriptures too.) Several things contributed to my healing process, which enabled me to take more of a leadership role.

On more than one occasion, I was present at a meeting where the men confessed and repented, on behalf of the church, for the way women have historically been treated. Some of them have had a change of heart about the role of women in leadership, moving from a belief that women were supposed to be "under" men in the church, to recognizing that we can work together, side by side. As they have wept and asked for forgiveness, the women present have felt profoundly liberated.

I've also had the privilege of being part of various national leadership groups and teams, having been invited to join in my own right, not just because I'm Tony's wife. As the men in these groups have treated me as their equal—valuing my contributions, treating me with honor and respect—I have come to a place of acceptance that I have a role equal to that of the men.

Jesus said this:

> You know the saying, 'Four months between planting and harvest.' But I say, wake up and look around. The fields are already ripe for harvest. The harvesters are paid good wages, and the fruit they harvest is people brought to eternal life. What joy awaits both the planter and the harvester alike![11]

It's true. The harvest is ready. We don't need to wait. All that's needed are more workers. It's time for women to bring their full contribution. As Psalm 68:11 (NASB) says, "The Lord gives the command; the women who proclaim the good tidings are a great host."

Discussion Questions

1. What challenges do women in your faith community face? Are these challenges internal (only in their minds) or external (your community limits their role)?

2. Felicity shared things she was taught when she became a believer. Were you taught them too? Are any of them correct?

3 Do you believe women want a greater voice? If not, why are they content to remain silent?

4. How can you encourage women to step out more?

Chapter 3 Notes

1. Tony and Felicity Dale, George Barna, *Small is Big!: Unleashing the Big Impact of Intentionally Small Churches,* (Carol Stream: Tyndale House Publishers, 2009, 2011); Felicity Dale, *An Army of Ordinary People,* (Carol Stream: Tyndale House Publishers, 2010).

2. "Yoido Full Gospel Church," *Wikipedia,* accessed November 2013, http://en.wikipedia.org/wiki/Yoido_Full_Gospel_Church.

3. Luke 10:2.

4. Roy Middleton, "John Wesley's Legacy – Perfectionism and Women Preachers," 2003, accessed November 2013, http://www.middletome.com/microsoftwordthelegacyofjohnwesley2.pdf.

5. Brett C. McInelly, *Everyday Revolutions: Eighteenth-century Women Transforming Public and Private,* (Newark: University of Delaware Press, 2008), 142.

6. George Orwell, *Animal Farm,* (Orlando: Harcourt Brace & Company, 1945), 118.

7. Kevin Giles, "The Biblical Argument for Slavery: Can the Bible Mislead?," *The Evangelical Quarterly, Vol. 66.*

8. 1 Corinthians 14:28.

9. 1 Corinthians 14:30.

10. 1 Corinthians 7:1.

11. John 4:35-36.

PART TWO

A WOMAN'S PLACE

LANA is a mother of four girls—ages seven, six, and three-year-old twins. Despite the rigors of being a fully involved mom, she wanted to make an impact for the Kingdom of God in her neighborhood. Lana lives in a suburban community on the affluent Marin Peninsula of California. Lana and her husband, Phil, teamed up with two other Christian families, hoping to reach their neighbors for Jesus. The families meet regularly to review how they are doing "up, in, and out"— "up" in their relationship with God, "in" their relationship with each other, and "out" in their relationship with neighbors. God put it on their hearts to host several neighborhood parties each year. They've had pumpkin carving parties, Cinco de Mayo celebrations, Easter egg hunts and Mother's Day get-togethers. The idea is to love their neighbors in a way that develops authentic friendships. Through these events, they have met "people of peace"—people who have a spiritual interest, or are drawn to the Jesus they notice living in others. As a result, a number of their new friends are meeting Jesus. Some have been baptized and are even taking their families to church or Bible studies.

CHAPTER 4

A TIME AND PLACE FOR EVERYONE

By Peggy Batcheller-Hijar

What does it take to see movement in any society? According to Peggy Batcheller-Hijar, it takes an immense thrust of energy.

Peggy is on the team of women who initially conceived the idea for this book. She has experienced many different phases in her life—from being a single woman to married, then divorced, and now remarried. She's raised young children; she's been an empty nester. Vocationally, she works as a nurse, while also functioning apostolically in her region.

Sharing from her personal journey, Peggy describes some of the struggles she has faced as a woman leader. Her story will resonate with many people, and all of us can learn from the principles she shares about the role of both genders.

Often, people say that women are too busy to spend significant time doing Kingdom work. But if we want to see the kind of harvest we all long for, it's going to take all of us, both women and men, co-laboring together.

Recently, I watched a program on public television about the women's movement called, "Makers: Women Who Make America: The Story of the Birth of the Modern Women's Movement."[1] It brought back many thoughts and emotions. I watched with intrigue, remembering that fiery season, remembering how the spiritual principles I'd been taught in regard to gender roles seemed so challenged during those years.

During the '60s and '70s, when this movement was in its infancy, I was a young adult. As a new believer in Christ, and a devoted follower of Jesus, I began to study the Scriptures diligently, desiring to have a strong faith and a deep understanding of Christian beliefs and biblical teaching. I was taught that women were not to speak or teach in the church. Women were instructed to wear head coverings during our meetings, and if we had questions, we needed to ask our husbands at home, not publicly in the church.

I remember watching the feminist movement struggle to take form. Women of all backgrounds and ages were marching and declaring their independence, burning bras, making a statement of their newfound freedoms. I cringed in disgust at this defiance of my scriptural principles, and I judged those women who were upsetting the world—or at least my world—and challenging the foundations of my Christian principles. Little did I realize how this movement would transform our culture, changing forever the way we view women's place in society.

Forty-some years have passed since the early days of that movement, and I've lived through many different seasons. Watching that program in amazement, I wanted to experience those times with different eyes and a different heart.

Who were these women participating in the early days of the movement? What did they want to accomplish through that march? Were they rebels, visionaries, haters-of-men, atheists, morally deviant women? I couldn't turn away from the television. My heart longed to hear their hearts, to understand the real issues behind their battle cries.

The biggest revelation I received in watching the program was that it takes a strong thrust of energy to change a person's life—stronger yet to change a culture, society, or nation. As a spaceship shoots out of this atmosphere into outer space, it takes strength and power to get beyond the pull of gravity. In the same way, as I watched those thousands of women marching, carrying signs, and proclaiming their freedom and equality, I saw the huge thrust of energy it took for them to achieve what they did. They made a stand, and their voices were heard.

There were other things I understood in a new light. The sexual revolution occurred simultaneously and colored the women's movement to a certain degree. Additionally, some women took things to an extreme and exhibited hostile attitudes toward men. Because some of the motives and results of the movement had a morally corrupt or antagonistic basis, many, especially those in the church, rejected the whole movement. The basic needs the women demanded were often overshadowed by controversy.

With the perspective time brings, I listened again to the words the women were speaking. They insisted on: "equal pay for equal work" and the privilege of being recognized for a job well done; release from the expectation put upon many women that giving sexual favors was the only means of ascending the corporate ladder; freedom from sexual/domestic abuse and human trafficking. I understood, possibly for the first time since the '60s, that most of these women weren't looking to overpower the men of the country. They simply wanted justice, fairness, and a chance to experience equality.

Some women back then seemed to overreact to many issues, but for change to happen, a strong thrust had to occur. It was a time of transition for women in our culture then. I believe it is a similar time of transition now, as our culture ushers women into more areas of leadership. This is not about seeking power and control, or overriding the rights of others. It is a call for equalization, respect, and honor—both in the secular world, and in the Christian church.

Telling Our Story

A very practical lesson I've learned through the years is the importance of telling our story. My story consists of many twists, disappointments, revelations, and growth in the Lord—just like many of your stories.

I grew up in a family of eight—six boys and two girls. Early on, I learned the unspoken rule that "boys are better," and that, as a girl, I had to compete with the boys at their activities to gain attention, approval, and acceptance. This understanding of boys are better later transferred into my marriage and church life as well. As young believers, my husband and I were biblically taught and trained with a religious understanding that reinforced my childhood beliefs about gender.

My husband and I both practiced man's authority over woman, and with my previous family upbringing, I had the mistaken belief that my husband, solely because he was a man, was better than I was at almost everything. Even though he verbally told me I had value, as the years passed, I failed to see it in myself. I took opportunities to be vocal in our small groups and in our church gatherings. I had the freedom to sing with the worship team, pray in groups, and grow in my spiritual walk. But inside, I felt I always had to compete, was never good enough, and could not stand on my own opinions.

My core belief was that my husband had to lead me, and I had to have his approval and permission in all I did to make sure I was doing it correctly. It was understood that I had to do ministry with him to have any value, and he was always the one in control. As the years went on, I trusted my own judgment less and less, and doubted I could hear the Lord on my own. Our marriage was becoming increasingly difficult, and my trust and faith in who I was before the Lord wavered.

Despite years of counseling and support, my marriage eventually failed. It was a very difficult time, bringing me much devastation and discouragement. It seemed that persons convicted of stealing and murder found more grace and forgiveness from the church than a divorced woman. But through it all, God worked in my heart.

God's love and forgiveness continued to encourage me, and I received many promises from his Word that led and directed me. A few close, believing friends stuck by me, listening and praying with me through those dark times. My faith in Jesus continued to grow as I welcomed again his payment for my sins through his death and victory on the cross and glorious resurrection. I felt refreshed and alive as he told me I could dream again, and that I could believe and trust him for my past, present, and future.

During that time, I also had the privilege of participating in an interactive website (LK10.com) for house church planters and leaders that my friend, John White, hosted.[2] As a recently divorced woman, I wasn't sure how other leaders and pastors would welcome me, so I was initially tentative in my participation. As time went on, I read more of the posts, responded to some, and found great encouragement and affirmation. During the next nine months, the interaction I had with John—and others who participated in the discussions—lightened my heart and gave me greater confidence in myself, first as a child of God, then as a church leader, and (coincidentally) as a woman. John was faithful to include me in discussions, introduce me to other church planters, and inspire me to walk with the Lord, listening to his heart.

I continued to interact with the other Luke 10 participants, tested some of their suggestions, and found that God was increasingly restoring my heart and reigniting gifts he had imparted to me in the past. Local church leaders encouraged my growth into apostolic leadership. The community from the Luke 10 website affirmed me as a viable church planter just starting to spread her wings. I gained strength and hope as I learned to walk closely with the Lord, listening to him and obeying what he said. I stayed in close relationship with other believers as we met in our homes and in the virtual world of the Internet. As a result of my growing confidence, I was invited to have a stronger voice in the organic church community in our local area, and throughout the state.

Later that year, I attended Tony and Felicity Dale's "Labor Day House2House Conference" in Dallas, Texas. John had introduced me to many leading men and women in the organic church movement through his web page, and now I had the opportunity to meet them face-to-face. They had been following my posts, watching me grow in my role and responsibilities in the Lord, and praying for me. At the conference, many wanted to assist and bless me on my journey.

Up until that time, I had lived what I believed was a life of failure, self-doubt, and low self-esteem—with an inability to move forward in my spiritual gifts apart from my husband. But these leaders encouraged me to proceed with what God had instilled in me. For the first time in my life, I accepted who I am—a wonderful daughter, full of hope and expectation, with a voice to be heard (not hidden behind my husband's ministry or calling).

I call my brothers in the Lord who have supported me on this journey my "Baraks."[3] They challenge me to accept the leadership God has given me and to fight the battle alongside them. Through their encouragement and direction, I grew in my responsibilities in the region where I live. I offered counseling and provided direction on listening to the Lord and starting simple churches. I met with both men and women for coffee, meals, conferences, and fellowship. I've seen God do amazing things in bringing freedom to many who are struggling to find their place in the church.

After a few years of being single, I sensed God's nudge to consider marriage again—to seek a partner in life and ministry. But I struggled with what it would look like compared to my previous marriage. Would I suddenly need to submit to my new husband's authority and give up my renewed sense of gifts and calling?

I heard God speak to my heart, saying, "Peggy, you have been healed these last five years from hurts in your past. But you have one more area that needs healing, and it is in your relationships—especially with a husband."

A few months after hearing God say those words, I met, fell in love with, and later married Richard. Richard has come alongside my ministry and we minister to men and women together. In the beginning of our marriage, I could feel myself falling into the old patterns of self-doubt, minimizing myself and my calling, and wanting to place him as leader. But as Richard came to know me better, he took extra care to step aside and to reinforce my relationship with the Lord. In those early months, he would often say, "I'm a step to the left and a step to the rear." God, in his grace, is bringing us into a very mutual relationship of equal submission, equal encouragement and heart of service to the Lord, and a unique relationship with God and with each other.

Self-Limitations and Barriers

I learned many things during this transition in my life. Through the years, I had minimized and belittled what God had given me, believing that if I just promoted and supported my husband and his calling and ministry, God would bless me. I now believe I was deceived (perhaps ignorantly, but often blatantly) by people who had a limited view of the entire Kingdom of God, people who continue to demand that God's daughters take a backseat in ministry.

I don't believe we are all called to be leaders, but we *are* all called into freedom.

Many women, though free, are living under the same bondage I once faced. They have been devaluing who they are in the body of Christ, believing they have to be behind or below the men in their lives—either men who are leaders in the church, or in their marriages and relationships. We have put up barriers in our own lives that prevent us from becoming all that God has called us to be.

These barriers stem from many sources:

- Our own lack of self-esteem
- Lies we have believed about the order of authority of men and women
- Lies we have believed about our value in our Lord Jesus
- The belief system we inherited from our family background and upbringing
- Religious teachings that have wrongfully kept women from being all God created them to be
- Barriers women have placed on themselves that limit their growth and confidence in the Lord
- Cultural status that lowers a woman's place, either in society or in the church
- Husbands, brothers, and men who hold a dominating position over spouses, daughters, and women

Men are not to blame entirely for the diminished place women have in the church or in society. We have grown up in a culture that has minimized women for centuries. Women have accepted a lower place for generations. However, I believe God himself is stirring up this generation to right the wrongs we have believed about the place of women in family relationships, society, and in the church. It is a time of renewal, restoration, and recovery for women.

God has given us the privilege and responsibility of following him, walking alongside him, and obeying as he speaks. So how do we live our fullest for him through every stage of life?

Single Women

A single woman has a difficult place in our culture today, especially in our churches. These women may take on many different appearances—young, elderly, divorced, widowed, single parent, college student, businesswoman. They have a unique living arrangement since there is no spouse to offer support. With a single income, they often need to rely solely on themselves for living expenses, insurance, and raising children; sometimes they are the only caregivers of elderly parents too. This can be a lonely season; these women need our encouragement and support.

What about single women in leadership? In traditional church settings, leadership generally rests on one man—the pastor—with possibly a board of other men in leadership over a congregation. But God is changing our church culture and our way of meeting, not only to "allow" women to step up and be active, but to actually participate in leadership. There are still some who disagree and criticize this way of thinking, but I believe a new wave of the Holy Spirit is ushering women, whether single or married, into leadership roles.

Women have been given gifts of evangelism, teaching, discipleship, prophecy, and leadership. God himself wants women to be courageous, rather than cowering in fear. He stirs the hearts of men and women to be bold in working together.

We, as the body of Christ, should not only recognize these single women and their specific needs, but also support them in finding their places in church and their calls in the Lord. We break new ground for women as we recognize their leadership roles in the church, as well as in society.

Women in Organic Church Communities

As more and more followers of Jesus leave the traditional setting of "legacy" churches to find communities of believers in more organic settings, new opportunities of freedom and responsibility arise for all members of the body of Christ. House church communities offer responsibility and a greater variety of leadership roles for women as they grow in confidence as daughters of the King.

Women in apostolic work are well-recognized in organic church communities. They start new churches in neighborhoods, workplaces, and day care facilities—without the need of financial backing, denomination support or approval, or being "sanctioned" by men or other leaders. The simplicity of walking with Jesus and following what he says has given them a new freedom and joy as they share their lives with others.

More opportunities also arise for mothers of children in the home. Moms and children are meeting together with other families in groups like Mothers of Preschoolers (MOPS) for encouragement and fellowship. Other parents meet in parks, take turns caring for each other's children, or meet for prayer and encouragement while the children play together. In our changing society, it has become more acceptable for women to take leadership roles and share responsibility with their husbands for the spiritual needs of their families.

Mothers also start churches. There are times in a mother's life when her priorities are focused on raising children—but even then, God uses them in Kingdom work. When we think about the simplicity God is bringing back to church structure, we have less and less requirements of what "church" is to look like. Jesus said, "Where two or three are gathered in my name, there I am in their midst."

Two or three may not fulfill some believers' expectations of what an entire congregation should consist of, but it can be the beginning of a strong community of believers. Mothers of children have been known to start churches as they walk together with other women, and transfer their heart and passion for the Kingdom of God to others.

A New Awareness for the Next Generation

About three years ago, I had the privilege of meeting with 11 other women for a weekend to pray about the place of women in the church, especially in leadership roles. The younger women, the twentysomethings who participated, amazed me. They shared the struggles of being single, providing their own income, and the difficulties of college life. They felt alone at times, not knowing what lay ahead for them.

But these women didn't seem to have the same barriers and old belief systems that I struggled with through my lifetime. They experience far less discrimination against women than we did during the 1970s and '80s. Through their stories, I could see how God is at work, revealing his freedom for women in this new season. In this generation, he is bringing a fresh revelation of his purpose for women in his Kingdom. The freedom for this younger generation to move into leadership is helping us all transition into a new mindset and understanding of women's roles in the church.

No longer is a single woman expected to sit back, hoping to someday marry, so she can have a voice through her husband. No longer are married women expected to serve the vision of their husbands while having no call on their own lives. God desires his entire body to be fully alive and functioning. We can be more than we ever imagined. Some of us women who are older, and who have broken through our own barriers, can set an example for those coming behind us. God calls "Baraks" to come alongside us. With both their help, the coming generations of men and women called to serve side by side will find strength and freedom to complete the task Jesus has given us—to take the Gospel of Christ to every person.

Discussion Questions

1. What kind of messages did you receive about women while you were growing up, both from the church and from society? Were these modeled or taught?

2. Are you still living in the light of what you were taught about gender roles in the church when you first became a believer?

3. What will change if you rethink some of your old paradigms concerning women?

Chapter 4 Notes

1. "Makers: Women Who Make America," PBS Video, accessed November 2013, http://video.pbs.org/video/2336932877.

2. http://lk10.com, accessed November 2013.

3. The story of Deborah and Barak, Judges 4–5.

CALLED by the LORD into ministry at age 12, Pam Durso figured, "that must mean missions." However, during college at Baylor University, her eyes were opened to many vocational ministry options. Her heart's desire was to become a teacher, so she enrolled in seminary, completed a PhD, and joined with a newly forming Baptist movement in 1990 that encouraged women in ministry. She currently serves as executive director of Baptist Women in Ministry, a non-profit organization that has championed women in ministry for 30 years. Her call is pastoral, but she describes herself as an encourager; she meets with many young women called to full-time ministry, and helps them along their chosen path, even when the barriers seem daunting. Pam understands the value of support from family, mentors, community, and peers. A particular delight of hers occurs annually in February, when Baptist churches throughout the country are invited to welcome women to their pulpits. In 2013, about 200 churches embraced the opportunity. Sometimes, this exposure is an impetus for churches to eventually add a female to their pastoral staff. Currently, there are about 150 clergywomen in the Baptist expression. Pam is a wise and patient change-agent, living out her values as a Baptist historian, academic, author, and theology professor.

CHAPTER 5

A WOMAN'S PLACE IS IN THE CHURCH

By Jan Diss

"Jan Diss" is a pseudonym for a gifted woman who works within a mainline denomination. She loves the institution that employs her, but could potentially lose her job if she was associated with a book promoting women in ministry.

Can women survive religious institutions? Is there a role for women in denominations where there is a pronounced "stained glass ceiling" for women in leadership roles? What can a woman gifted with leadership abilities do if God leads her to stay within an institution that restricts the use of her God-given gifts?

What Jan has done takes courage and determination. It's not for the faint of heart. But she lives an extraordinarily fruitful life, and has gained the respect of the church community at a national level. Her life is proof that God can use a woman anywhere.

My mother was a flannel shirt and jeans, ban-the-bra kind of woman. It was the 1960s when I first realized the stuff she was made of, but her family confirms she had been the same in the 1930s. Sometimes I imagine that my mom was Gloria Steinem's mentor, and that she had actually been the first to coin some of Steinem's words, like, "…no one knows what leadership has gone undiscovered in women of all races…."

Ah, mom. Her girls grew up learning about Marie Curie, Susan B. Anthony, Clara Barton, Amelia Earhart, and Elizabeth Cady Stanton. Female scientists, activists, and pilots really lived. They were not feminist fairy tales. I'd been taught that women really could accomplish greatness, so the women's lib hype in the '60s confused me a bit.

Hadn't our gender already proven ourselves? Mom led the PTA, the children's Sunday school department, her garden club, and every other arena her world encompassed. She was an indomitable force in our household. Dad traveled for business, and Mom made clear and usually wise decisions about everyday life. I grew up believing that women could be leaders in the institutions of family, education, society, and church—just about anywhere they chose. That was the world I knew.

It took many years and much disillusionment before I came to believe no such world existed for most women in the 1960s, '70s, and '80s. This realization first dawned on me as an adult when I became part of a conservative denomination where leadership seemed to be the special domain of men. I still remember being shocked when a respected seminary professor refused to give me any time after class because he "only had time for young preacher boys." At my first denominational meeting of local pastors, I was asked to either play the piano or take notes for the group. Through the years, though, I eventually found my way. For several decades now, I have learned how to function within denominational conservatism. Here are some of the lessons I learned.

LESSON 1: There seems to be a special category for single female missionaries.

Married women who are missionaries are often not recognized, except through the work of their spouses, but unmarried women are more likely to be acknowledged for their own work. Mother Teresa earned her voice through missionary service among the poor in India. When asked what she thought about the feminist movement among nuns in the West, she said, "I think we should be more busy with our Lord than with all that, more busy with Jesus and proclaiming his Word. What a woman can give, no man can give. That is why God has created them separately." Mother Teresa was not a feminist, nor did she seek to promote herself, yet she had a voice that echoed around the world.[1]

There are many other notable female missionaries. In 1822, Betsy Stockton, an African-American woman, was sent to Hawaii by the American Board of Missions. This made her the first single woman missionary in the history of modern mission, and she blazed the trail for others to follow. Fidelia Fiske was the first single missionary woman to Persia (now Iran). Presbyterian missionary Eliza Agnew, started a school for girls on the Island of Ceylon (Sri Lanka). She educated and loved on so many of her students she was nicknamed, "Mother of a Thousand Daughters." Lottie Moon was a tireless missionary to China. She made such an impact that Southern Baptists named their international missions offering in her honor. Whether working among the poor, ministering to orphans, or starting new churches, single women who are missionaries are often more acknowledged than their married counterparts, even when married women engage in the same activities.

However, there is another very opposite phenomenon that plagues single females, even missionary women. Some institutions will not allow single women to minister at all. They tell them to come back when they are married, and to wait until that time to serve. To make matters worse, they do not restrict single males in the same way. Our hearts bleed with women in this position, and we have no good words of wisdom, except do not allow your hearts to become bitter, and seek another route to ministry.

LESSON 2: Work hard for the sake of the Kingdom, not just to prove yourself as a woman.

In December 2011, the National Geographic Society gave its 10,000th grant to Dr. Krithi Karanth, a 32-year-old conservation biologist from India. She was interviewed about what it is like for her as a female scientist in both the United States and in her home country. She admitted that in both countries, women have to work 10 times harder than men do. Clearly, she is not the only person to observe this discrepancy, and it is no less true for women in ministry. For example, in evangelical denominations, how many seminary-trained women obtain paid ministry jobs after graduation as compared to men? In 2010, one national survey reported that 8 percent of evangelical congregations in the United States had a female as their principal leader.[2]

There really is a "stained glass ceiling" for women in ministry. The issue is not solely theological, but societal as well. Studies still show that male/female wage differentiation exists in most industrialized nations. Women earn less than men do, even when employed in the same positions. In the United States, until the early 1960s, newspapers published job listings for men in different columns than openings for women. The highest paying jobs were almost all specified for male candidates. In 1960, the Equal Pay Act declared it illegal to practice gender discrimination in wages, yet still today, women earn only 77 cents for every dollar that men earn. The female-to-male earnings ratio has not seen a significant annual increase since 2007.[3]

Women in paid ministry positions often experience another barrier. Institutions that prohibit female ordination, by default, also prohibit women from the clergy housing allowance exemption. In these cases, even if women on staff receive the same wage as their male counterparts, they are required to pay tax on a portion of their salaries that male ministers declare as tax-exempt.

Scripture includes all kinds of people in its work ethic—men, women, and even slaves. Hear the words of the Apostle Paul:

> Therefore, my dear brothers and sisters, stand firm. Let nothing move you. Always give yourselves fully to the work of the Lord, because you know that your labor in the Lord is not in vain.[4]

> Slaves, obey your earthly masters in everything; and do it, not only when their eye is on you and to curry their favor, but with sincerity of heart and reverence for the Lord. Whatever you do, work at it with all your heart, as working for the Lord, not for human masters, since you know that you will receive an inheritance from the Lord as a reward. It is the Lord Christ you are serving.[5]

There is a discipleship revolution happening among the world's least-reached peoples, and in particular, among Muslims. It is an approach called the "insider movement" that has resulted in new Christians continuing to retain their cultural and religious identity—to remain legally Muslim, and yet call themselves "Muslim followers of Christ." This controversial approach is clearly quite opposite to extracting new believers from their former cultures and relationships.

For decades, I have worked as an insider in the context of conservative Christian organizations. Changing the perspective of women's role in ministry from the inside has been slow and challenging. It is also a calling. Through the years, I have learned a critical lesson: there is room for those who will serve God with all of their heart, soul, mind, and strength, despite the pressures of injustice, lack of opportunity, and inequity.

LESSON 3: Women must mentor other women as leaders, not compete against them.

I have a confession to make. For many years, I tried so hard to prove that I was as good at what I do as any man in ministry that I did not pay attention to other women struggling around me. I had not been mentored by any women in the church, and concluded I was not responsible for mentoring other women either. Yet, as a new convert to Christianity, I longed for female mentors. I began sensing that I might find this connection I craved through biographies. After pointing to women in Scripture who were used by God, my pastor introduced me to women in modern history: World War II rescuer Corrie Ten Boom, who proved to me that modern Christian women could make a difference; Catherine Booth, who co-founded the Salvation Army; evangelist Aimee Semple McPherson, who founded the Foursquare Church; and Fanny Crosby, nineteenth century hymn writer. These were the women who mentored me and gave me the courage to become a leader.

All the while, however, I longed for other women to come alongside me, to struggle with me, grieve with me, experience my victories, and help me grow in wisdom and grace. I missed that support and encouragement when I first led a group, spoke in public, gave an address, graduated from seminary, accepted my first position at a church, organized my first large event, and so many more memorable occasions. Until a few years ago, I never imagined I was capable of giving back to other women who needed the same thing, but I could have been doing that all along. Today, I mentor women leaders because I want to give back out of my own journey. I work to keep women involved in ministry and growing as leaders, even during the years they have small children at home. It is my privilege to include other women in all of my ministry activities—wherever they can learn, grow, give back, and utilize their spiritual gifts.

Another reason some women are slow to mentor other female ministers is because Christian institutions are often closed organizations with limited opportunities for advancement. Closed organizations breed competition for scarce opportunities, which means that knowledge, information, and strategic relationships are guarded and hoarded instead of freely shared. Though it is against their basic nature, even women who prefer mentoring relationships can be shaped by the competition that is bred in closed organizations. The undercurrent becomes, "if there is room for only one female here, let it be me."

LESSON 4: Women leaders must learn to rely on biblical sources of authority.

It is less problematic for women to lead in simple (organic, house, basic) churches. Why? Because in these kinds of churches, the lines between clergy and lay ministers are blurred. Generally, there are no salaries, no hierarchies, and few titles. Nobody is called senior pastor, and everyone is a minister. Leadership is understood more by gift than by role, and it is more a verb than a noun. Leaders lead, ministers minister, apostolic individuals reproduce churches, and healers heal. Biblical leadership is practiced:

Each of you should use whatever gift you have received to serve others, as faithful stewards of God's grace in its various forms. If anyone speaks, they should do so as one who speaks the very words of God. If anyone serves, they should do so with the strength God provides, so that in all things God may be praised through Jesus Christ.[6]

This is not meant as a rebuke against functional leadership roles such as worship leader, youth minister, or children's minister, but it is a very different thing. When these titles disappear, women are more likely to be invited to lead according to their gifts, talents, and capacities.

LESSON 5: Appreciate men who care, and work closely with them.

Real gentlemen open doors for women, or so we were taught. Yet the doors women in ministry really need opened for them are doors of opportunity, respect, and credibility. We need courageous, gentle men to stand up, move over just a little, and make room for the female voice to walk by their side. Men like this have been present in my own life, and it has deeply mattered. First and foremost is my husband, who is truly the spiritual leader in my family. He is secure enough to be content when I flourish, and kind enough to care about my pain. He has helped me become who I am as a follower of Christ and a female minister. I immensely appreciate him. There are others I appreciate too—I call them men of grace. Here are some of the places I find them, and how I recognize them:

- Sometimes they say odd things like, "women and men," instead of "men and women." This lets me know they realize I am in the room. These men offer water to my soul, even when their attempts are awkward.

- They are appropriately sensitive about their hymnology, selecting gender neutrality where it makes sense. This also holds true for the language in their preaching. Usually, they are not aiming to be politically correct, but to be genuinely inclusive of both genders, or to contextualize Scripture in a meaningful way for the female half of the church.

- When I speak in their churches, they invite me to their pulpits or lecterns with them. They realize that I, too, need a place to keep my notes while I speak.

- They affirm my giftedness, and they never say, "For a woman, that wasn't bad." They converse with me about my thoughts and convictions.

Once, a male leader apologized to me, and to my friends, for how the church has so often excluded women from the Gospel of grace. This man is a hero. On the flip side, there are many stories that could be told about men who view women as a curse, a problem, or a tool of Satan. I prefer to remember, instead, the men of grace who choose to walk side by side with women, seeing us as vital partners in the Kingdom workforce.

LESSON 6: Learn to forgive well-intentioned brothers in Christ, even when their gender biases cause excruciating pain.

After decades of ministry, and a certain degree of earned leadership, I wish I could say that the system has changed. I would like to have emerged as a heroine whose work was so outstanding that it impacted how my organization made its decisions about women leaders. But that hasn't happened yet. As a matter of fact, it has actually become more difficult over time. As women have become leaders in other domains, such as business and politics, some mainline Christian organizations have asserted a strong defensive posture to make certain that church women keep their places. They have fortified the walls, narrowed or reiterated their positions, and assumed an even more watchful posture.

But what's a woman to do? Forgive, it seems; focus on our common commitment to become Christ-like. And when ministry becomes the cross on which our missions are crucified, we must cry out to the One who understands our pain, "Father, forgive them— they know not what they do."

These are the lessons I have learned. I remember how far the world has come since the day in which my mother's generation was raised, and I contrast that with all I have experienced in these decades as a woman seeking to serve God. I see his providence and it encourages me. He alone is in control, not man, and not woman. This brings me great hope.

Discussion Questions

1. What lesson from Chapter 5 was most relevant to where you are now in your journey?

2. Who have been the female mentors in your life?

3. Women: Are there men who have helped open doors of opportunity in the Kingdom for you? What difference has this made in your life?

   Men: Have you opened any doors of opportunity for the women in your life? What was the outcome? Are there more doors you could open for other women?

1) Seeking God in working with others, both male & female. This isn't a competition, working together is the goal.

2) Lisa, Morgan, Kaitlin, Pastor Ginny, PH

3) yes, Pastor Jim has made an enormous change in my life & has helped me grow closer to God

Chapter 5 Notes

1. Edward Desmond, "A Pencil in the Hand of God," December 4, 1989, *Time Magazine,* accessed November 2013, http://www.time.com/time/magazine/article/0,9171,959149,00.html.

2. "2010 National Survey of Congregations: Evangelical Protestant," accessed November 2013, http://faithcommunitiestoday.org/sites/faithcommunitiestoday.org/files/2010EvangelicalFrequenciesV1.pdf1.

3. "Income, Poverty and Health Insurance Coverage in the United States: 2012," United States Census Bureau, September 17, 2013, http://www.census.gov/newsroom/releases/archives/income_wealth/cb13-165.html.

4. 1 Corinthians 15:58 (NIV).

5. Colossians 3:22-24 (NIV).

6. 1 Peter 4:10-11 (NIV).

MEET ALI EASTBURN. At a women's retreat in 2006, a speaker posed a question that changed her life: "What can we do to change the world around us?" Ali became suddenly aware that there was far more she could do. The answer, however, was unexpected. "Sell your wedding ring and give the money to the poor." At that moment, her eyes were opened. She realized there are people in the world that don't have even the basic necessities needed to survive and she could help. Ali had spent the better part of her life shopping for significance, and her wedding ring was symbolic of her success. But when she sold the ring to help fund a well in Africa, God became more important than the "stuff" that once consumed her life. In 2007, Ali founded an organization called With This Ring in hopes that radical giving becomes a staple of the Christian community so that others' basic needs may be met. Women around the country have joined forces, and more than 1,000 rings have been donated. With This Ring is now funding wells in nine countries and counting. Ali Eastburn. Full surrender. Radical giving.

CHAPTER 6
CROSS-GENDER FRIENDSHIPS—
ARE THEY SAFE?

By Katie Driver

First Timothy 5:1-2 exhorts Timothy to "treat older women as you would your mother, and treat younger women with all purity as you would your own sisters." Somewhere in our church history, we lost sight of that verse. Today, it is often thought inadvisable for a man to have even a sisterly friendship with someone of the opposite sex. Who knows what problems it might lead to!

This has greatly impoverished the body of Christ. If men and women are genuinely going to co-labor together for the sake of the Kingdom, then we need a fresh understanding of how cross-gender friendships work out in practice. Obviously, we need to be wise, but our lives will be considerably enriched if the Victorian nature of these cultural taboos is lifted.

Katie Driver is no stranger to wholesome and pure cross-gender friendships. She has worked with men in many different capacities, often as their leader. Katie serves as an apostle—training church planters both here and internationally, bringing churches together for regional training, and coaching and encouraging church leaders across the theological spectrum who are interested in a more organic form of church.

Here, Katie offers her firsthand experiences with cross-gender friendships among Christian brothers and sisters, exploring a common concern: are they safe?

I am a happily married woman who often interacts with other men through various relationships. I have done so all of my life. I work with and alongside men far more than I do with women, whether through my job as a motorcycle instructor, or as a ministry leader, church planter, and mentor. I also work primarily with men when training and leading teams internationally, networking in my region and other countries, and as a trainer and coach in simple, organic, and missional church. The reason? In all these areas, men far outnumber women.

Are relationships between men and women—whether friendship, ministry, or mentoring—so complex and laden with issues that they will inevitably lead to inappropriate and even sinful connections? These relationships are certainly not encouraged, and they are highly suspect and scrutinized in most evangelical Christian environments.

I have strong, close, and honorable relationships with men in various contexts, and my husband has always been supportive and encouraging of these friendships. Relationships between men and women can be rich and full of rewards and benefits. To be clear, I'm *not* referencing the sexual phenomenon of "friends with benefits" that is a common activity in our society today. I'm referring to deep, abiding relationships across the gender divide that offer different perspectives and interpersonal dynamics, and can provide incredible blessings in life and ministry. However, these relationships do require a vigilant awareness of healthy boundaries, as well as regular and honest self-assessment.

God created us male and female, not just for procreation purposes, but to also live as co-laborers and family members—brothers, sisters, mothers, fathers. Galatians 3:28 expresses the goal of the Holy Spirit as he unites us as one body with Christ as head: "There is no longer Jew or Gentile, slave or free, male and female. For you are all one in Christ Jesus."

We are called as Christians to overcome fear with faith. We are not to be overcome by the world and its lusts, but are called to be more than conquerors through Christ and his power, where fear has no dominion.

Cross-Gender Relationships Lead to "Things"?

Many years ago, I remember sitting in a booth at a local restaurant with the pastor of a fairly large congregation. I had requested the meeting so I could present a plan for the start of a new ministry in the church. I excitedly laid out the vision, with all the details the Lord had given me, of starting a young adult church within the traditional church I was attending. The vision had developed throughout several months of listening to God and praying over the details. I had become more and more sure this was something I was passionate about, called to do, and capable of starting.

As I spoke, I watched the pastor's face and could tell he liked everything I was presenting. He nodded, smiled, and occasionally interjected, "That's great!" His positive encouragement spurred me on until I finally finished, sat back, and waited for his response with eager anticipation.

"Katie, this is fantastic!" he said. "I've been praying for something along these same lines, and yet never put it together like you have. It's exactly what I feel God wants us to focus on, and a way we can empower and encourage the young adults in our fellowship. I'm ready to launch this as soon as we can!"

I was momentarily elated as he continued, "Now, help me discern—who is the man in our church that could start and lead this ministry?"

I sat stunned. In fact, I remember having to consciously close my open mouth. I thought maybe I had misunderstood and clarified, "So you like my idea, but you don't feel I'm capable of leading it?"

Now it was his turn to look stunned.

"You? Well, no. It's a great idea, Katie…God's direction and all, but we need a man to lead it. Sorry."

"Why?" I asked.

"Because having a woman lead could complicate relationships. You'd be working with an all-male staff and young men in the ministry itself," he replied. "To be honest, I don't think women should be in leadership positions like this, especially where they work with men. It's not safe. Things could happen."

Of course he was referring to sexual "things" like attraction, flirtation, lust, and adultery. Yes, things can happen, but not just between men and women. Sexual misconduct can also occur between men (as we've seen recently with a few prominent male leaders who were having sexual liaisons with other men) or between women (as happened in a church I attended some years ago).

Control Doesn't Prevent Sin

As much as we'd like to try and protect ourselves from the pull of sin, the only remedy is the power of Christ, honest accountability, and maturing to the place where the flesh does not overcome the Spirit. Legislation and control by excluding a particular gender and outward appearances of "religious veneer" never have, and never will, keep sin from occurring. In fact, these things can actually encourage it in our reliance upon them to keep us safe. The more we rely upon outward and spiritually impotent constraints for our safety, the less we mature to a place where sexual sin and impropriety have no dominion over us. We are not called to control our environments, but to be wise, discerning, and to grow in maturity.

Once, when my husband and I attended a church planter's conference in Los Angeles, the leader of this particular denomination exhorted those present, asserting that pastors should "make sure they hire an old and unattractive woman to be their secretary." This way, they "wouldn't find themselves tempted into sin with someone they work with daily."

Sadly, I'm sure this is not unusual advice given to men in ministry, but it is only addressing the environment and not the maturity of the leader. There is plenty of teaching that says men can't be expected to have healthy friendships and working relationships with women, and vice versa. The message communicated with this advice is that we are just too weak, vulnerable, immature, sinful, and at the whim of every commercial Satan sends our way. The solution offered is that it's better to control the environment and keep us separate from one another than to mature! It's the Christianized version of the Muslim burka—out of sight, out of mind. Unfortunately, this actually keeps us from maturing and only enables us to be at the mercy and dominion of our flesh. We miss out on the interaction God intends for us to have in the richness of male and female relationships. Our segregation limits the full activation of the whole body of Christ, where men and women function in a multitude of roles and capacities alongside each other.

Jesus, Paul, and Women

Jesus didn't avoid relationships with women, even with those women who had a history of sexual sin and proclivity. He also didn't avoid being alone with women. His disciples thought it strange, but Jesus wasn't frightened or inhibited from interacting and even befriending women of all reputations. Yes, he was fully God, but he was fully man as well. If we are to follow the example of Jesus in all things, doesn't that include the example of his relationships with women, which was even more taboo in his day and culture than our present times?

The Apostle Paul didn't avoid female relationships either. From his writing, it is easy to see that he valued and enjoyed the women in his life. They were his respected co-workers in ministry whom he cared about in friendship and worked alongside in the trade of tent-making. Married women, single women, old and young women—Paul easily refers to the women in his own life. Priscilla, Phoebe, Mary, Junia, Tryphaena, Tryphosa, Persis, and Julia are but a few he mentions in the book of Romans alone.[1] Instead of telling us to avoid male and female relationships, he reminds us to choose what rules us. In situations where we may be tempted to sin, Paul advises, "Do not let sin reign in your mortal body so that you obey its lusts."[2] In Galatians 5:16 (NASB), he puts it this way: "Walk by the Spirit, and you will not carry out the desire of the flesh."

Close Cross-Gender Friendships

Many years ago, I belonged to a group that met once a month and focused on the area of missions in my city. The group was almost exclusively made up of men who were mission pastors at churches, or leaders of para-church organizations in the city. Occasionally, a woman came as an assistant to someone, to give legal advice for non-profits, or as a visiting missionary from overseas. The purpose in gathering together was to encourage one another in ministry and friendship, and allow members to showcase their particular ministry in mission opportunities.

I was invited to attend these meetings by a man I had recently met. We both led small mission ministries that took teams to minister internationally in short-term missions. We had much in common and enjoyed the synergy that happened when we met together, discussing the topic of mission work. We felt encouraged and strengthened by one another, understanding the challenges of our particular area of ministry. We became good friends and true co-laborers, and soon our spouses became a part of our friendship.

When my friend and I attended these citywide meetings for mission professionals, we sat together quite comfortably and with obvious familiarity with one another. We often noticed there was some tension with my presence—awkwardness in many men who would speak to my friend about his mission's organization, but would not recognize my presence at all and walk away as if I were invisible. My friend would get sideways glances of disapproval, while I would get ignored. When my friend was not there, I usually sat by myself and seemed to have an invisible line around me that said, "Danger! Woman by herself! Don't go too close!"

Thankfully, some men have not been afraid of getting too close to me, and they have been true friends and treasured brothers. One such man is James Engel. Jim came as a speaker to the mission professionals group I belong to. I accidently sat at his table, not knowing who he was, or that he was the guest speaker. I was simply looking for company and friendly interaction. We immediately hit it off through our conversation, and found an affinity for one another in a short time. Jim is known across evangelical circles for his contribution in creating a scale that examines the decision-making process of becoming a Christian, called The Engel Scale.[3] Jim became a dear friend and mentor to me, listening and encouraging my heart for mission work and nontraditional church. My being a woman was never awkward for Jim, or for his wife, Sharon, who welcomed our friendship and fellowship. Our normal place to get together was at Jim and Sharon's home, where Sharon would often make us a pot of coffee and then leave us to our discussions. A few years later, Jim and I traveled to Cyprus (without a chaperone or spouses) to act as consultants to a ministry based in the Middle East. It was a fantastic time in our friendship and for me personally in ministry. Jim will always be loved and appreciated in my life as a man who saw me not only as a capable woman, but also as a fellow ministry worker and friend.

It can be incredibly lonely to be a woman in traditional and predominantly male ministry areas. If a woman's ministry does not fall into one of the familiar categories—women and children's ministry, prayer, worship, etc.—the ostracism that occurs can test the best of us in stamina and commitment to the call on our lives. There have been many times through the years the battle has worn me down, and I've wondered if it was worth pressing forward in the calling God has given me. If not for the support of my husband and a few good men, I'd have quit a number of times and missed out on the incredible experiences that come when we persevere and overcome.

One such time came on a trip down to a seminary in southern Brazil. The night before I was to speak and lead the conference, our host pulled me aside and warned, "Katie, I want you to know that most of the men at this seminary won't accept a woman teaching them from the pulpit. You should be prepared for their rejection."

I responded, "Well, I don't have to speak. I didn't come down here to cause you dissention and problems! We will have one of the guys speak instead."

"No, I want you to speak," he replied. "I will deal with any fallout, but I want you to get up there to teach and minister. I'm only telling you now so you'll be prepared for what might happen."

I wrestled all night with God on this one. I argued, whined, and complained until I finally felt God give me peace and tell me he would take care of it all. I was to be obedient, to speak and minister as he directed. I was to talk about Jesus—his power, his mission— and he would back me up.

The time came, and sure enough, some of the male seminarians left the room as I began to speak. A few turned and spoke to each other, ignoring me as if I was not speaking; many more communicated through their body language that they were not happy with me. I turned my focus to the group of men who were a part of the team we brought down (my husband being one of them) and the brother who hosted us, taking in their encouraging smiles and nods. I felt and saw their love, support, and encouragement, and it strengthened me to continue. The Lord came in powerful ways and validated my speaking and ministry, as only the One who holds all the authority can.

At the end of a powerful week, during our goodbyes to the seminary students, a man stood before me with tears rolling down his cheeks. He asked me to forgive him for the way he had treated me during the first few times I spoke.

"I never knew a woman, let alone a woman who wears makeup and jewelry, could minister so powerfully in the Spirit. I am a changed man, and I want to release and support my two daughters and wife to minister in the way God wants them to minister. He has shown me I have been wrong in thinking women shouldn't minister to, or with, men."

If the seminary host had bowed to cultural pressure, I would not have spoken and ministered during the week. I would not have had the opportunity to trust the Lord in his capacity to use me in the way he purposed with the support of the men around me. Nor would the brother who asked for my forgiveness have had the opportunity to be set free from his religious bigotry and release his wife and daughters with a blessing.

It's not always easy, though, and doesn't always end well. I have had friendships with men whom I valued as true brothers and friends come under incredible pressure to break off further contact with me. This pressure came from pastors, mutual friends, and occasionally, spouses, who were not comfortable with the friendship between us. A woman once accused me of having adulterous thoughts toward one of my male friends. When I vehemently denied her accusations and asked for specific things that would support them, she broke down in tears and confessed her own illicit thoughts toward a male co-worker. If she had those thoughts, she assumed I must too! I also have had many brothers who simply cannot even consider me, as a woman, in friendship or as a co-worker in ministry alongside them. Even if they don't agree with limiting women, they are not willing to place themselves in a position where they may be targets for suspicion or allegations.

However, some are willing to open the door to cross-gender friendships and co-laboring relationships. Two examples of such men come to mind: Church Multiplication Associates (CMA) founder and director Neil Cole, and his ministry partner, Mike Jentes.

I often function as host, promoter, and trainer at Greenhouse Training weekends with CMAResources.[4] At one of these events, a group came from another state to attend a weekend I was hosting in my city. After the event, I continued in contact with the group leader so I could encourage him and his small church plant on the journey they began. I invited him to host a Greenhouse event in his area to help others learn more about this paradigm of simple, organic church.

CMA typically asks regional Greenhouse trainers in close proximity to host the workshop because it's easier to provide help and mentoring once the Greenhouse weekend is over. Since I fit the bill on two counts—not only as a regional trainer for the area, but also already mentoring this particular leader—I was asked to be one of the trainers for their event. I was excited and looking forward to continuing the relationship.

Neil later called to report that the group was "uncomfortable with a woman being one of the trainers, and wanted a man instead." I took it on the chin, although it hurt and the rejection stung. It wasn't something I was unfamiliar with. Neil apologized, ranted a bit about the injustice of it, and did his best to promise it wouldn't happen again. I knew it would, and said so. It was my reality; now they were sharing in it. CMA placed me instead with a different Greenhouse event that was to take place on the East Coast, and both Neil and Mike went out of their way to convey their confidence in me to the host.

It didn't help. I received a phone call from Neil again. This time, he was even angrier as he related how this second group also insisted on not having a woman as their trainer.

Neil and Mike are men who stand up for something and someone they believe in, and they did not give up. Within a few months, I was speaking at a Greenhouse event in another location. They continue to bring me to the frontlines as much as possible, promoting my role as trainer, regional coach, networker, and mentor. They have made my gender a nonissue, and their support and unwavering belief in me has strengthened me and encouraged me to keep ministering.

Where are the Baraks?

When Barak proclaimed that he would not go to war without Deborah, it had multiple effects:

- It encouraged and empowered Deborah herself in her role as judge.

- It sent a powerful message of support for a woman in leadership and validated her authority to those unaccustomed to women in such a role.

- It proclaimed that Barak and Deborah were a team, and together they would fight the battle and become victorious.

- Since we know Deborah was married, and possibly Barak too, it set an example of a man and woman working together in God's purposes who were not married to each other.

- It propelled another woman named Jael to bold action. She sealed the Israelites' victory by killing Sisera.

An Important Issue

Another question that often arises is whether it's appropriate for a woman to mentor younger men (or a man to mentor younger women). A mentor is defined as a person or friend who guides someone who is less experienced. In order for mentors to have any effect or be valuable, they must build trust, engage in authentic relationship, be good listeners, and be aware of the issues in the life of the person being mentored. They also need to model and share practical life experiences and have a history of credibility. It makes sense then, that a mentor will usually be older. In regard to gender, men and women have much they can learn from each other.

I spend a lot of time mentoring and coaching men (and some women too). I'm used to the "raised eyebrow look" when guys see that their motorcycle coach or ministry mentor is a woman, and I accept the reality that I will have to be 10 times better than their expectation to gain credibility. (A male counterpart in my same role is given instant credibility until he proves otherwise.) However unfair that is, an advantage I have in being a woman mentor and coach is that most men have a certain affinity for women and are not threatened by them. If I come alongside someone as a sister, mother, or (at my age) grandmother, it feels natural and is usually accepted. I also get the opportunity to change preconceived notions based on gender. We can achieve greater unity in the body of Christ by getting to know one another personally, and we can't do that to any great degree if we aren't willing to reach across the gender line.

There are many issues surrounding this highly controversial topic, including propriety, wisdom, misunderstanding, misinterpretation, setting boundaries, and protocol for crossed boundaries. But male/female friendships can be so rewarding and fruitful, we do ourselves, and the church, a great disservice by avoiding them. There is a lot of risk and potential for sin in many areas of our lives. But we are called to live in dependence upon Christ at all times, for all things, without trying to control our lives in such a way that we don't need faith. My hope is that we can begin the discussion and truly look at how we can mature together. We do not need to live under the mantle of fear that immobilizes and hobbles us with the "what ifs!"

Discussion Questions

1. Do you have any Kingdom friendships with the opposite sex (apart from your spouse)? I am working on it

2. Who are they and how have they enriched your life? If you answered no, why not? What is your fear? —

3. How could you be more open to those of the opposite gender that would allow for Kingdom growth? I need to ask God

4. What will you do to allow God to create more of those relationships in your life? yes

---

Chapter 6 Notes

1. In Romans 16, ten of the 29 individuals Paul mentions are women. That's 34 percent. These women appear in active roles. Phoebe was a deacon and a "patroness" (Greek *prostatis*), a word that has definite leadership connotations. Priscilla, along with her husband, Aquila, hosted a church in their home. Mary, Tryphena, and Tryphosa were the Lord's workers. Junia was an apostle.

2. Romans 6:12 (NASB).

3. James F. Engel & William A. Dyrness, *Changing the Mind of Missions: Where Have We Gone Wrong?*, (Downer's Grove: InterVarsity Press, 2000), 110-101.

4. Church Multiplication Associates, http://www.cmaresources.org, accessed December 2013.

PART THREE

THE GENDER DEBATE
AND SCRIPTURE

JULIA ROSA MACHADO has been an evangelism powerhouse and effective church planter in her home country of Brazil for 20 years. Women in Brazil are typically limited to traditional roles in ministry: supporting a pastor/husband, heading up a women's ministry. Not Julia Rosa! She stepped outside of the norm into the fullness of her gifting. With a strong sense of mission and boundless energy, she reaches into economically poor areas and showcases the riches of knowing Jesus Christ in simple and profound ways. Few men or women can keep up with her pace and drive in bringing as many people as possible to faith in Christ. She boldly proclaims salvation and the cost of becoming a disciple. She reaches many by obediently praying for the sick and needy. Julia is an apostle who touches the hearts of Brazilian men, women, and whole families, bringing freedom and building the Kingdom.

CHAPTER 7
CREATED IN GOD'S IMAGE—
MALE AND FEMALE

By Felicity Dale

The New Testament passages that are often referenced to limit the role of women in the church stand against the general tenor of Scripture as a whole. In these few, isolated verses,[1] the Bible apparently allows the subjection of women. But the general trend of the Scriptures, especially the New Testament, points toward women being equal co-heirs and co-laborers alongside their male counterparts. Therefore, we are faced with a choice: shall we isolate the challenging passages and follow them without taking the rest of Bible into consideration? Or, do we take into account the principles demonstrated throughout the Scriptures, most notably by Jesus himself?

A vibrant young lady had been taking a particularly active role in her small group Bible study. One day, after discussing the topic of church, the group concluded that their gathering probably fit the biblical definition of church. From that day on, the young woman stopped participating. When asked why, she replied, "As a woman, I'm supposed to keep silent in church."

Our understanding of what the Scriptures teach regarding a woman's role in the church matters. It matters to women. But it also matters to the entire body of Christ. The church is robbed of the complete expression and beauty of Christ when half its members do not function fully.

God Lets People Choose

I'd like to propose a theory. God, in his incredible love and mercy, opts to work within the constraints humanity creates for him. Here are a few examples:

- God desired to speak directly to all Israelites at Mount Sinai when he gave them the law,[2] but they were so afraid, they asked him to speak only through Moses.[3] God honored that request.

- God desired for the Israelites to be a Kingdom of priests,[4] but in the end, only the Levites were obedient and were set aside to serve God.[5]

- It was not God's will for Israel to be governed by a king,[6] but once the nation had chosen to go that route, God worked within that context.

- The argument could be made that God didn't want a temple built for him; it was David's desire to build him one.[7] Yet God chose to bless the temple that Solomon built.

God did not desire a patriarchal society. But once mankind had fallen, and men subjected women under their control, God, in his loving mercy, worked within that framework.[8]

The New Covenant that Jesus ushered in through his death and resurrection changed everything. For Christians, it reversed the effects of the Fall back to the goodness of the created order. Under the New Covenant, God's laws are written on our hearts, and we can all know him, from the least to the greatest.[9] Jesus himself is our Lord and King. We have become the temple of the living God,[10] holy priests.[11] And under the New Covenant, we are all one in Christ.[12] God's original design was for men and women to work together in the Kingdom.

God's Original Plan

We see God's original intention in creating men and women revealed in Genesis 1:26-28:

> Then God said, 'Let us make human beings in our image, to be like us....' So God created human beings in his own image...male and female he created them. Then God blessed them and said, 'Be fruitful and multiply. Fill the earth and govern it.'

God is Spirit, without gender. It takes both male and female to represent God. Males on their own do not fully reflect the image of God; nor do females. God designed it so both genders would get their identity and value from him alone, a model of unity and co-regency—ruling by serving together. There's no evidence in the first two chapters of Genesis that Adam and Eve had distinctive roles based on gender.

When God saw that man needed a companion, he didn't create another man—he created woman. Together they were to co-reign and care for creation as stewards, multiplying and filling the earth. Hierarchy is described between man and animals, but there is no hint of man being above woman.[13] If God had wanted Adam to rule over Eve, surely this was the ideal time to have given that command. Instead, one might say that woman, created last, is the culmination of God's creation.

A Masculine God?

Most of the imagery concerning God in the Bible is masculine, and God is consistently referred to as "he." But not exclusively. God is also described as a mother eagle,[14] like a woman in labor,[15] as a mother with children,[16] and Jesus describes himself as a mother hen.[17] Even one of the names of God, El Shaddai, usually translated "Almighty," is also said to have a literal meaning of "breasted one," one who nourishes and sustains.

Wisdom (*sophia*) in Proverbs is clearly feminine, and is described as being present at creation.[18] In fact, it's hard to separate "Wisdom" from the person of Jesus in how she is described.

> I was appointed in ages past, at the very beginning before the earth began.... When he marked off the earth's foundation, I was the architect at his side... his constant delight.[19]

Although Jesus took on a male body, he was born a bastard child in a despised ethnic group, humbling himself for our sakes.

God is Spirit, without a body and therefore non-gendered. The members of the Godhead are different, yet complementary. Some of the attributes ascribed to the Holy Spirit are ones often associated with feminine qualities—helper, comforter, counselor—and the fruit of the Spirit includes love, kindness, gentleness. The Godhead is gender inclusive, not exclusive. The body of Christ is best represented by both genders, functioning fully in the gifts God has given them.

The Origins of Patriarchy[20]

The consequences of the Fall were a disaster for mankind.

When God confronted Adam and Eve in the garden following their meal of forbidden fruit, rather than fess up and take personal responsibility, Adam blamed first God and then Eve: "It was the woman you gave me who gave me the fruit and I ate it."[21] Eve, on the other hand, is accurate in her perception of what had occurred and her part in it: "The serpent deceived me. That's why I ate it."[22] God's curse on the serpent follows: "Because you have done this, you are cursed....And I will cause hostility between you and the woman, and between your offspring and her offspring. He (Jesus) will strike your head, and you will strike his heel."[23]

We can see how this curse has played out in more ways than one. Does Satan have a special hatred for women? When you look around the world at how women have been gang-raped, tortured, aborted, mutilated, beaten, starved, and brutalized in every evil way at the hands of evil men, it is tempting to think so.

After God curses Satan, he turns his attention to Adam and Eve. God curses the ground and tells Adam, "All your life you will struggle to scratch a living from it." Interestingly, some of the results of the Fall God describes seem to coincide with the individual way the genders were created. Adam, who was formed from the dust of the earth, now has to work cursed ground; Eve, who was formed from Adam's side, will be now ruled over by her husband.

"Yet your desire will be for your husband, and he will rule over you"[24] has been used to justify the relegation of women to "second-class" status throughout history. But here's the real question: Is this statement by God descriptive or prescriptive? It has certainly proven to be true (descriptive), and helps us understand the mistreatment of women throughout history. But is it what God intended (prescriptive)? Was God cursing Eve, or was she suffering the natural consequences of her actions?[25]

God never—nowhere in Scripture—*commands* men to rule over women. The Bible begins with an affirmation of women. Yet men, even some whom we respect in other ways, by observing nature from a human vantage point, have devalued women for millennia:

...women are probably degenerate and cowardly men. (Plato)[26]

The male is by nature superior and the female inferior, the male ruler and the female subject. (Aristotle)[27]

What is the difference whether it is in a wife or a mother, it is still Eve the temptress that we must beware of in any woman... I fail to see what use woman can be to man, if one excludes the function of bearing children. (St. Augustine)[28]

As regards the individual nature, woman is defective and misbegotten.... (St. Thomas Aquinas)[29]

> Blessed are you, Lord, our God, ruler of the universe who has not created me a woman. (Prayer recited every morning by traditional Jewish men)

> Even though they grow weary and wear themselves out with child-bearing, it does not matter; let them go on bearing children till they die, that is what they are there for. (Martin Luther)[30]

Would anyone say these attitudes are Christ-like? Yet they demonstrate an attitude toward women that has haunted the female half of humanity down through the centuries.

Women Throughout the Old Testament

If God, as some say, has chosen to use men in leadership, then (despite a highly patriarchal society) he picked a remarkable number of women to demonstrate his purposes. God is always consistent. He would not go against his principles and use women in leadership if he had specifically forbidden it or prescribed that women should be ruled by men. As we look at the Bible, we see God working with women throughout its pages:

- Women played a crucial role in the founding of the nation of Israel.[31]

- For many years, a woman held the highest office in the land.[32]

- On more than one occasion, women rescued the nation.[33]

- They are described as prophets,[34] sometimes changing the course of history.[35]

- Two books are devoted to the story of women.[36]

- Women built city walls,[37] stood up for what is right,[38] and took a stand for justice.[39]

In none of these examples is there any hint that God was only using these women because he couldn't find a man to do the job. Furthermore, despite the fact that women were not usually mentioned in Jewish genealogies, Jesus' ancestry[40] specifically mentions women, even some rather "disreputable" candidates. Perhaps God is demonstrating that he can work through whomever he chooses, including these women who rose above their circumstances, against great odds:

- Tamar, who masqueraded as a prostitute to her father-in-law, Judah, in order to obtain justice[41]

- Rahab, a prostitute, who rescued the spies sent by Joshua to scout out Jericho[42]

- Ruth, the Moabitess, who gave up her own people in choosing to follow her mother-in-law

- Bathsheba, who committed adultery with King David, but was the mother of Solomon[43]

Freedom for the Captives

God's desire for liberty and freedom from oppression are writ large through the pages of Scripture and are a major theme of God's interaction with his people. When the Children of Israel were in bondage to other nations, when they called on his name, he found a way to set them free.[44] God spoke through Moses to Pharaoh, "Let my people go!"[45] He made provision in his laws to deal with slavery[46] and debt[47] so people weren't permanently in bondage.

When Jesus announced his mission at the beginning of his ministry, he used a passage from Isaiah[48] about healing broken hearts and setting captives free.[49] As we see from the account of Jesus' life in the Gospel of Luke, this often included women. If Jesus came to set captives free, then the church, above all places, should be the place where freedom is proclaimed and experienced.

Who have been among the most enslaved throughout history? Who have been among the most exploited and abused? Women. Our mission should be the same as Jesus', to proclaim release to the captives and set free those who are oppressed.

Ultimate Revelation

God has been progressively revealing himself throughout history. If we want to know what God is really like—the ultimate revelation of the Father—we need look no further than Jesus, the visible image of the invisible God, who reveals the character of the Father by his actions, attitudes and words.[50]

Jesus refused to be bound by the conventions of his day, especially in his treatment of women. Jesus treated all women with dignity and respect. He regarded them as friends in a society that viewed them as inferior. There's no hint of superiority in his attitude toward them. We never hear him speak in a condescending way to them—in fact, some of his deepest theological conversations occurred with women.[51] He didn't cringe when a prostitute wiped his feet with her hair,[52] or flinch when Mary anointed him.[53] He encouraged Mary to adopt the posture of a disciple.[54] He entrusted the message of his resurrection to women.[55]

Even in a society that was highly patriarchal, Jesus featured women in his stories.[56] He gave illustrations that women would relate to,[57] never told a story where a woman was the "villain," and publicly honored women as examples to follow.[58] He welcomed their children; he defended their rights.[59] He befriended and discipled them—a group of women accompanied Jesus for much of his ministry.[60]

In a casual read through the New Testament, it's easy to miss the role of women. There's an interesting character I like to call Mrs. Zebedee (although her name was probably Salome),[61] the mother of James and John. It's worth looking more closely at her life. Mrs. Zebedee accompanied Jesus from Galilee:

> And many women who had come from Galilee with Jesus to care for him were watching from a distance. Among them were Mary Magdalene, Mary (the mother of James and Joseph), and the mother of James and John, the sons of Zebedee.[62]

To back up a bit, the story of Jesus leaving Galilee for Jerusalem began in Luke 9:51: "As the time drew near for him to ascend to heaven, Jesus resolutely set out for Jerusalem." Luke 10 continues with the story of Jesus sending out the seventy "other disciples."

There's no way to prove it, but it seems likely that Mrs. Zebedee and the other women mentioned were among those Jesus sent out two by two, praying for the Lord of the harvest to send workers out into the harvest. They found "people of peace." They healed the sick and proclaimed the good news of the Kingdom. They reported back to Jesus how even demons were subject to his name. And Jesus told them that they, too, had authority over all the power of the enemy.[63]

If we look at Matthew's version of Jesus' life, his final journey from Galilee to Jerusalem begins in chapter 19. We know Mrs. Zebedee was with Jesus in chapter 20, because she plays a key part in the story, asking Jesus if her two sons could have positions of prominence in his coming Kingdom. The women were probably there at the raising of Lazarus, the triumphal entry into Jerusalem, for much of Jesus' final teaching, and for other key events that occurred toward the end of Jesus' life.

We often assume, when the Gospels refer to the disciples, that women were not present. For example, Mark's version of Jesus' teaching on leaders being servants does not mention women.[64] It would be easy to assume that only the 12 disciples were involved. However, Matthew's version fills in the details: "Then the mother of James and John, the sons of Zebedee, came to Jesus with her sons" and requested they be allowed to sit at his right and left hand in his coming Kingdom. In response, Jesus seized this "teachable moment" to talk about servanthood.[65]

Mrs. Zebedee was there when Jesus died. She watched as his body was taken down from the cross and as Joseph of Arimathea laid it in his own tomb.[66] If Mrs. Zebedee was indeed Salome, she purchased burial spices and prepared them on the evening of the Sabbath with Mary Magdalene and another Mary.[67] She also may have been present at the empty tomb when an angel told the women that Jesus had been raised from the dead.[68] And she was probably with Mary Magdalene and the other women as they told the 11 disciples that Jesus had risen.[69]

Did Mrs. Zebedee leave for home immediately after Jesus' resurrection? Or did Jesus reveal himself to her along with the others who accompanied him from Galilee?[70] Did she "tarry in Jerusalem" until the Day of Pentecost? Was she one of "the women" mentioned to be among the group of 120 in the upper room when the disciples cast lots to choose a replacement for Judas?[71] Was she there when all the believers were gathered together in one place, and the Holy Spirit came like a rushing, mighty wind, and they were all filled with the Holy Spirit?[72] Did she rejoice as 3,000 people became believers that day? Was she part of the early church described in Acts 2?

I'd like to think so.

But what about the rest of the New Testament? The church was born into the context of God pouring out his Spirit and working through both men and women (Acts 2:17-18). All believers are called to be a royal priesthood and ambassadors of the Kingdom. We find women apostles,[73] prophets,[74] and teachers.[75] Women evangelized.[76] Every church that is mentioned as being in someone's home includes a woman.[77] Paul called several women co-workers or workers for the Lord.[78] And when he lists spiritual gifts, none have gender restrictions—we have examples of women in many of the roles.[79] Women obviously played an active part in all that went on.

As Paul put it in the letter to the Galatians, "There is neither Jew nor Gentile, slave nor free, male nor female, for you are all one in Christ Jesus."[80] This verse doesn't just apply to our standing in God's sight, but in other areas too. Although there are still battles to fight, generally within the Western church, racial discrimination is no longer considered acceptable; slavery is no longer in existence. Yet the church still permits gender discrimination.

We, the body of Christ, are supposed to be Jesus' hands and feet here on earth, the outworking of the Kingdom of God to the world. We know how Jesus behaved toward women. We know there will be no gender bias in heaven.

Let's live that way now.

Discussion Questions

1. Discuss the relationships Jesus had with a) his mother, b) the woman at the well, c) Martha, and d) Mary Magdalene.

2. How do you think those women responded to Jesus? How could the modern day woman respond to Jesus' interaction? How would it make a difference in the present day church?

3. The whole tenor of the Scriptures is toward liberty. Does anything need to change in your treatment of others to reflect this?

Chapter 7 Notes

1. 1 Corinthians 14:34-35; 1 Timothy 2:11-15.
2. Exodus 19:9.
3. Exodus 20:19.
4. Exodus 19:6.
5. Exodus 32:26-29.
6. 1 Samuel 8:5-20.
7. 2 Samuel 7: 5-7; Acts 7:49-50.
8. For further exploration of this topic, see *Beyond the Curse: Women Called to Ministry* by Aida Besancon Spencer.
9. Hebrews 8:8-12.
10. 1 Peter 2:4-5.
11. 1 Peter 2:5.
12. Galatians 3:28.
13. Gilbert Bilezikian, *Beyond Sex Roles,* (Grand Rapids: Baker Academic, 1985), 20.
14. Deuteronomy 32:11.
15. Isaiah 42:14.
16. Isaiah 49:14-16.
17. Luke 13:34.
18. Proverbs 3:13-18; Proverbs 4:4-9; Proverbs 8; Proverbs 9.
19. Proverbs 8.
20. For further exploration of this topic, see *History and the Triune God* by Jürgen Moltmann, and *The Fall of Patriarchy: Its Broken Legacy Judged by Jesus and the Apostolic House Church Communities* by Del Birkey.
21. Genesis 3:12.
22. Genesis 3:13.
23. Genesis 3:15.
24. Genesis 3:16 (NASB).
25. According to a number of authors (e.g. Joyce Baldwin in *The Role of Women,* and Sandra Payne in *A Call to Women*), the tense of the verb "to rule" is a simple future tense, not an imperative.
26. Plato, *The Project Gutenberg eBook of Timaeus,* translated by Benjamin Jowett, 2008, eBook #1572.
27. Aristotle: *The Politics Book 1,* section 1254b.
28. Epistles 243, 10 quoted in Brown, Augustine of Hippo.
29. *Summa Theologica,* Article 1, Question 92.
30. http://www.archive.org/stream/ grisarsluther04grisuoft#p age/144/mode/1up in Luther by Hartmann Grisar.
31. Sarah (Gen. 17-25), Rebecca (Gen. 24-29), and Rachel and Leah (Gen. 29-35).
32. Deborah (Judg. 4–5).
33. Deborah and Jael (Judg. 4–5), and Esther.
34. Miriam (Exod. 15:20).
35. Huldah (2 Kings 22).
36. The books of Ruth and Esther.

37. The daughters of Shallum (Neh. 3:12).

38. Abigail (1 Sam. 25).

39. Zelophehad's daughters (Num. 27:1-8).

40. Matthew 1:1-16.

41. Genesis 38.

42. Joshua 2.

43. 2 Samuel 11-12.

44. Judges 2:10-18.

45. Exodus chapters 5-10.

46. Exodus 21:1-11.

47. Deuteronomy 15:1-18.

48. Luke 4:18-21.

49. Isaiah 61:1.

50. Colossians 1:15.

51. John 4; John 11:20-28.

52. Luke 7:36-39.

53. John 12:1-6.

54. Luke 10:38-42.

55. Matthew 28:5-10.

56. Luke 15:8-10; Luke 18:1-5.

57. Luke 13:21; Matthew 9:16.

58. Mark 12:41-43; Matthew 26:6-13.

59. Matthew 19:3-8.

60. Luke 8:2-3.

61. In the Matthew version of the crucifixion, three women watching as Jesus hung from the cross and breathed his last are mentioned: Mary Magdalene, Mary the mother of James and Joseph, and the mother of James and John (i.e., Mrs. Zebedee). The Mark version of that same story also lists three women: the two Marys and Salome (Mark 15:40). It seems likely that Zebedee's wife's name was Salome.

62. Matthew 27:55-56.

63. Luke 10:1-19.

64. Mark 10:35-45.

65. Matthew 20:20-28.

66. Luke 23:55.

67. Mark 16:1; Luke 23:56.

68. Mark 16:2-8; Luke 24:1.

69. Luke 24:10.

70. Acts 13:31; 1 Corinthians 15:6.

71. Acts 1:14.

72. Acts 2:1-4.

73. Romans 16:7.

74. Acts 21:9.

75. Acts 18:26.

76. John 4:39.

77. Romans 16:3-5; Colossians 4:15; Philemon 1:2.

78. Romans 16:3; Romans 16:6; Romans 16:12.

79. Romans 12:6-8; 1 Corinthians 12:7-11, 1 Corinthians 12:27-28; Ephesians 4:11-13.

80. Galatians 3:28.

IN 2008, at age 26, Sherilyn Sheets learned the hard way that instead of following your dreams and asking God to bless them, the only way to see any dream accomplished is to follow the Dreamgiver. Two years later, Sher followed God, by faith, to Chicago and moved specifically into a neighborhood that was home to a lot of uncelebrated, lonely, and vulnerable people. While her only goal was to be a good neighbor, the favor and fruit she experienced resulted in the establishment of a restorative non-profit called JUSTembrace. But it's more than that. It's a lifestyle—a movement spreading across the country. JUSTembrace equips people to live lifestyles of restoration by offering hospitality, generosity, and inclusivity. By modeling these values in a neighborhood packed with thousands of homeless, addicts, mentally ill, isolated, and marginalized people, Sher and volunteers empower others by meeting practical needs and building relationships. JUSTembrace hosts dozens of yard events, house parties, foot clinics, and birthday parties each year, inviting people to celebrate life together. They easily impact more than a thousand people yearly; parties generally involve a few hundred guests and many dozens of volunteers. By modeling the biblical example of early Christians, JUSTembrace has provided a sense of home for the truly homeless in the midst of Chicago.

CHAPTER 8
BUT JESUS DIDN'T HAVE FEMALE DISCIPLES, RIGHT?

By Frank Viola

One of the questions our team of women is often asked is this: "Why didn't Jesus have female disciples? Surely he could have had six men and six women."

But Jesus did have female disciples. Luke's Gospel provides this account:

Soon afterward Jesus began a tour of the nearby towns and villages, preaching and announcing the Good News about the Kingdom of God. He took his twelve disciples with him, along with some women who had been cured of evil spirits and diseases. Among them were Mary Magdalene, from whom he had cast out seven demons; Joanna, the wife of Chuza, Herod's business manager; Susanna; and many others who were contributing from their own resources to support Jesus and his disciples.[1]

Mary (mother of Jesus), Mary (mother of James and Joseph), Salome, Mary (sister of Lazarus), and Martha were all followers of Jesus too. In a culture where women had few (if any) rights, it is extraordinary that the Gospels record so many names of women who followed Jesus.

When our team of women looked for someone to write about women in the life of Jesus, Frank Viola immediately came to mind. A popular conference speaker, blogger, and prolific author, Frank has been writing for several years (almost poetically) about a group called "The Women" in the life of Jesus. He is a champion and encourager of women in ministry.[2]

Jesus treated women differently than any other Jewish teacher of his day. Women played a prominent role in his ministry.

This chapter aims to unpack that statement. It will give you a peek into how Christ viewed women during his earthly life, and how he views them today—for he is "the same yesterday, today and forever."[3]

It must first be said that women in Jesus' day were treated poorly both by the Jewish and Roman worlds. They could not receive an education. They had no voice in their marriage, and they were limited to a special court in the Temple that was inferior to that of the men. A Jewish man was not supposed to talk to a woman in public. If he did, it was considered a shame. Jewish women were to be seen in public as little as possible. The prevailing view of women in the Jewish mind was that they were regarded as private property.

But Jesus of Nazareth turned all of this on its head.

In the following list, I'm deliberately not giving the Scripture references. The reason is because I want to challenge you to re-read the Gospels, and as you do, ask what role women played in the life and ministry of Jesus. By doing so, you will see each point below emerges in the narrative.

A Survey of Women in the Gospels

- Elizabeth and Mary (not Zechariah and Joseph) were the first to receive the news of the coming Messiah. They were also the first to prophesy about the Christ child.

- Anna the Prophetess helped pave the way for the coming of the Messiah, preparing those who were waiting for his arrival.

- Jesus came into the world through the womb of a woman. For this reason, Mary, the mother of Jesus, is among the most beloved, honored, and respected women who ever lived. She shows us just how vital women are to God's eternal plan.

- It was unheard of for women to be listed in a Jewish genealogy. But the Gospels include women in the genealogy of Jesus.

- John the Baptist introduced Jesus to the people of Israel as "the bridegroom." God chose a woman—the bride of Christ—to depict the church, whom Christ loved and gave his life for.

- Jesus spoke to a Samaritan woman in public and told her some of the most amazing things about God that he ever shared with anyone. The disciples were shocked that he spoke to her in public. Not just because she was a woman, but because she was a Samaritan. Jews weren't supposed to speak to Samaritans.

- Jesus often used women in his parables and made them heroes. Think of the widow and her mite, the woman and the lost coin, the persistent widow and the unjust judge, the 10 virgins with oil in their lamps, etc.

- Jesus allowed a "sinful woman" (whom many believe to have been a prostitute) to kiss his feet. She also unbound her hair, which was a scandalous gesture in that day. Yet Jesus allowed her to love him extravagantly in the house of a Pharisee.

- Jesus allowed an unclean woman to touch him. As a result, she was healed.

- Jesus became the defense attorney to a woman caught in the act of adultery. As a result, her life was saved.

- Jesus healed the daughter of a persistent Gentile woman and gave her one of the highest compliments he paid anyone. Her faith was peerless in his eyes.

- Jesus is said to have "loved" two women who lived in the little village of Bethany (Mary and Martha) along with their brother Lazarus. Mary and Martha were among Jesus' closest disciples and were probably the most prominent women in his life, next to his mother.

- Jesus entered into a woman's home (Martha's) and taught another woman (Mary) specifically, along with his other disciples. For a Jewish teacher to come into a woman's house to teach was unheard of.

- Jesus allowed a woman (Mary of Bethany) to sit at his feet and learn from him. To sit at a person's feet was to take the posture of a disciple. So Jesus allowed Mary to learn from him the same way that he allowed his male disciples to learn from him. Jesus allowed Mary to take up the space that was only designated for men. (This is why Martha objected so strongly.)

- Jesus said that Mary of Bethany would be mentioned and remembered wherever the Gospel would be preached. An amazing honor. This was after Mary anointed his body for burial with a rare and expensive perfume.

- Jesus defended a woman on two occasions when her act of love and devotion were ridiculed and rebuked. Her sister, Martha, (and later, Judas and the other the disciples) rebuked Mary of Bethany. In both cases, Jesus rose to Mary's defense.

- A group of women followed Jesus along with the Twelve. The women also took care of his needs out of their substance. Luke, in the Gospels and in Acts, calls this group of female disciples "The Women." Jesus was the first Jewish teacher to have women disciples. And for a Jewish woman to leave her home and travel with a Jewish teacher was not only exotically rare, it was considered scandalous.

- Jesus spent his last week on earth (before his resurrection) in the home of a woman. He stayed with Mary, Martha, and Lazarus in Martha's home in Bethany.

- Jesus' female disciples stayed with him during his death, proving themselves to be more faithful than most of his male disciples. With the exception of John, Jesus' male disciples deserted him during his darkest hour.

- Jesus' female disciples were the first to show up at his tomb to care for his body.

- The first eyes that witnessed the resurrected Christ were the eyes of a woman (Mary Magdalene). Ironically, during the first century, a woman's testimony was of no use in a court of law. Yet God in his wisdom allowed a woman to be the first witness to the greatest miracle ever accomplished.

- In the whole of Jesus' public ministry, there was nothing in his words or deeds that indicated any concern to restrict the spiritual service of women.

Key Takeaways

Jesus came into a world where the cards were stacked against women. The ways he engaged, conversed, healed, and recognized them in his teachings were radical for his culture, but they were second nature to Jesus.

The Son of God was keenly aware that the image of God was both male and female (hearkening back to Genesis 1), and his life and ministry reflected that awareness. Remember, Jesus is the human face of God. So his opinion of women reflects God's opinion of women. Consequently, anytime women are oppressed or suppressed on the planet, the Lord would seek to liberate them.

Jesus is the greatest liberator in the universe. And freeing women to their God-given calling is one of the things he does best. Among other things, this would include the following:

- In the spirit of Mary Magdalene—the first woman to set eyes on the resurrected Christ—women are free to testify to the good news of Jesus and his resurrection.

- In the spirit of Mary, the mother of Jesus, women are free to fulfill God's will and calling, saying, "Be it unto me according to your Word."

- In the spirit of Mary of Bethany, women are free to worship Jesus Christ extravagantly. And they are free to sit at his feet as disciples, along with his male followers.

- In the spirit of Anna, women are free to prophesy by the Holy Spirit. In this way, women are called to serve as spiritual priests along with men, because they are part of the priesthood of all believers, and they, too, possess the Spirit.

- In the spirit of the Canaanite woman who persisted in her request for Jesus to heal her daughter, women are free to press into the Kingdom of God and wrestle with God until they receive his blessing.

- In the spirit of the women who traveled with Jesus—Mary Magdalene, Joanna, Susanna, and others—women are free to follow the Lord wherever he goes and serve him out of their substance.

- In the spirit of the Samaritan woman whom Jesus met at Jacob's well, women are free to pioneer evangelism and church planting initiatives.

The call to follow Jesus as a full-fledged disciple and the call to serve God goes out to all women, just as it does to all men.

So to my dear sisters (and brothers), I say—go and follow the Lamb wherever he leads.

More on this subject by Frank Viola:
"God's View of a Woman," frankviola.org/view.htm
"Rethinking Women in Ministry," frankviola.org/role.pdf

Discussion Questions

1. What insight do you get from the list Frank gives in regard to God's releasing women into their calling?

2. What action(s) in this list do you find revolutionary for Jesus' time and why?

3. For women: Which of the women mentioned do you most identify with?

4. For men: What is your next move in conquering cultural bias about women like Jesus did? When will you do this?

Chapter 8 Notes

1. Luke 8:1-3.

2. Frank Viola has written numerous books on the deeper Christian life, including *Jesus: A Theography* (co-authored with Leonard Sweet), *Epic Jesus, Revise Us Again, From Eternity to Here,* and *Jesus Manifesto.* His blog, "Beyond Evangelical," is rated as one of the most popular in Christian circles today: http/frankviola.org.

3. Hebrews 13:8 (NKJV).

TILLIE BURGIN of Arlington, Texas, is a model of servant leadership and contagious vision. Her influence has shaped literally thousands of lives. Tillie had a distinguished career as an educator. She and her family were missionaries (with the Southern Baptist Foreign Mission Board) for a decade. She wondered, "If we can do missions in Korea, why can't we do missions in Arlington?" Mission Arlington was birthed in prayer to meet the physical, emotional, intellectual, and spiritual needs of the community. The results are staggering. A Bible study outreach to one apartment complex has grown to more than 300 outreach locations for "simple churches" in the city. Mission Arlington/ Mission Metroplex also offers full-scale assistance. For example, 5,000 are assisted monthly with food and basic household needs. They offer emergency supplies, free medical and dental care, camps, after school care, transportation to school and work, counseling—and the list goes on. More than 143,000 volunteer hours were logged in 2012 alone. Tillie is now in her mid-70s and has been executive director for nearly three decades. She believes that every life has significance, and she has lived out those values with vision, commitment, and faithfulness.

CHAPTER 9

LEARNING CHRIST FROM ONE ANOTHER—
Can A Gathering Be Open & Participatory If Only Men Speak?

By Jon Zens

When our team chose who we wanted to tackle the challenging passages about women in the New Testament, Jon Zens was an obvious choice. A theologian and scholar for more than 35 years, he's done a thorough study of Pauline epistles, particularly as they relate to women.

The two main passages Jon discusses in this chapter have been used to limit the role of women in the church for centuries. Often, the English version is taken literally, without any regard to the original meaning in the Greek. This has had disastrous consequences for many women. In some of the stricter churches, women are not allowed to speak during the meetings. In some denominations, women are not permitted to "teach or have authority" over a man. This means they cannot teach in adult Sunday school, and are not allowed any role where they influence the congregation in a strategic way. In other denominations, women are not allowed "ultimate authority." They live a life of limitations, simply because of their gender.

If women of integrity believe that God has set men over women, that men are specifically designed to lead and women to follow—they may not like it, but will most likely submit to God's apparent guidance in this matter. But suppose this isn't true. What if the Scriptures that apparently limit women can be translated (with equal integrity) in a different way that is consistent with the overall message and tenor of the Bible and true to the original Greek? Perhaps Jon's interpretation of the challenging passages can shine some fresh light on old misconceptions.

From roughly 250 AD onward into modern times, it was assumed that women were barred from teaching in settings where men were present. This assumption was fed mainly by two New Testament passages: 1 Corinthians 14:34-35 and 1 Timothy 2:11-15.

Examples of the dogmatism of this biased position could be drawn from many sources, but here is one from 1709 in England:

> Still our Apostle is directing Timothy how persons should and ought to manage themselves in the Publick Assemblies, and particularly how Women ought to behave themselves at the Time and in the Place of Worship; let, says he, the Woman in your Assemblies learn in silence with all subjection to the better Sex; for I suffer not a woman to teach publickly, and to usurp authority over the man, to whom God has given Authority over her, but rather, according to her Duty, let her learn in Silence.[1]

To the contrary, there is considerable evidence in the New Testament that portrays the sisters as participating fully in ekklesia (church) life. And yet, this great bias is manifested whenever these two passages are used to silence female believers.

Spirit-Gifted Sisters Prophesied in Public

On the Day of Pentecost, Jesus came to his Bride in the person of the Holy Spirit and a striking event took place, as recorded in Acts 2. People from numerous nations had gathered in Jerusalem for this special festival. The 120 brothers and sisters who had been in the upper room prophesied and proclaimed the wonderful works of God in various foreign languages. Some felt that those prophesying were filled with too much wine. Peter pointed out that it was the wrong time of the day to be drunk. He then cites what Joel had foretold long ago would come to pass:

> 'In the last days,' God says, 'I will pour out my Spirit upon all people. Your sons and daughters will prophesy. Your young men will see visions, and your old men will dream dreams. In those days I will pour out my Spirit even on my servants—men and women alike—and they will prophesy.'[2]

What happened on this glorious day must be viewed as formative and normative for the body of Christ on earth until this Gospel age ends. Both genders are liberated to prophesy for the Lord. There are no restrictions or qualifiers. It does not say or imply that only men can prophesy publicly. Nor does it say or imply that women can only prophesy privately or to other women and children. This is especially important when it is remembered that Paul strongly desired prophesying to be central in the gathering of the ekklesia.[3]

When great minds try to sidestep the public prophesying of women, their suggestions are puzzle pieces that do not match the New Testament picture. To illustrate this, John Piper's view dictates that women should not speak publicly in any way that might "snuggle up to teaching." Thus, his conception of what it means for a woman to "prophesy" is non-public and very limited in scope. He posits:

> The fact that a Christian wife and church member, according to Acts 2:17, may 'prophesy' implies, at least, that she may often have ideas and insights that a wise and humble husband and pastor will listen to and adopt.[4]

This sounds like an opinion born out of a narrow agenda, not a conviction formed by listening to the voices of the men and women depicted in Acts 2.

There is additional New Testament evidence to support that women prophesying in public was an accepted—even encouraged—practice in the early church. Among the commentaries on 1 Corinthians, there is virtual consensus that a mixed gathering of saints was in view in chapter 11. The passage echoes Acts 2 (men *and women* prophesied) and reflects the centrality of prophecy that Paul wished to happen when they came together as an ekklesia.

The outcomes of prophesying mentioned in 1 Corinthians 14 are "building up, exhortation, comfort, encouragement, instruction and learning." Thus, it is clear that since Paul was speaking of a time when the whole ekklesia came together, he envisioned the sisters being part of the expression of Christ that would result in "teaching, instruction, and learning."

There was nothing in Paul's flow of thought in 1 Corinthians 11-14:33 that would suggest only males could prophesy. Instead, everything Paul stated was gender inclusive: "When you come together as an ekklesia...each and every one of you has a song, a teaching, etc. You may all prophesy one by one..." (paraphrase). To use 1 Corinthians 14:34-35 as a trump card to cancel out the participation of the sisters revealed in so many other places (especially in the immediate context) is a very jaundiced way to interpret Scripture. I will address these verses shortly.

"Teaching" in the New Testament

Traditionally, we tend to think of "teaching" in terms of a person presenting material to others who are listening. However, New Testament perspectives would expand our narrow conception of this matter considerably.

Broadly speaking, believers came together to partake of the Christ within each other. Paul contrasted the Ephesians' former way of living with their new life by reminding them, "You have not so learned Christ."[5] In the New Testament, "learning" is not about gathering brute knowledge, but about going deeper in a Person—"growing in the grace and knowledge of Jesus Christ."[6]

Teaching is much bigger than a teacher/listener context. For example, Paul revealed that saints "teach and admonish one another" when they sing of Christ together.[7] So when the Lord gives a song to a sister to share with the assembly, she is contributing to the "teaching/learning" that is continuously taking place in the ekklesia in a variety of ways.

The writer of Hebrews exhorted recipients of the letter, saying: "You have been believers so long now that you ought to be teaching others. Instead, you need someone to teach you again the basic things about God's Word."[8] Not everyone will have the specific gift of teaching, but the whole body will be involved in the broad privilege of sharing Christ with one another. This will come by both women and men prophesying in a manner that results in instruction and learning.

Much more light could be given from the New Testament showing how believing women were active from the Day of Pentecost, when Christ's life exploded on the earth. We would do well to remember Psalm 68:11 (NASB): "The Lord gives the command; the women who proclaim the good tidings are a great host."

In his book, *Bonding: Relationships in the Image of God*, Donald Joy makes the pivotal point that both male and female must express Jesus together in order for the "image of God" (who is Christ!) to be present:

> We are always impoverished when a single sex group meets, discusses, and makes decisions, since only one part of the full-spectrum personhood seems to be present. So where urgent decisions are being made, we surely want both sexes speaking.[9]

Let's examine briefly, then, the two passages used to restrict female disciples. I must stress that what follows is a crisp summary of many lines of thought that are detailed in my book, *What's With Paul & Women? Unlocking the Cultural Background to 1 Timothy 2.*[10]

Before coming to these two scriptural contexts, we must understand that there is a huge assumption on the part of those who would silence women. This view assumes that the very act of a woman teaching a man is inherently a wrongful deed that violates "male headship." But nowhere is there a shred of biblical substantiation for such an extreme position. From both Testaments we glean the active role of women as presenters of God's will to his people:

- Deborah, a prophetess, judge, and wife, sat by her palm tree and made judgments as men and women came to her for counsel in applying the Mosaic Law to their lives.[11]

- King Josiah sent a male envoy to the prophetess and wife, Huldah, after the Book of the Law was discovered. She gave them (and ultimately, Israel) the Word of the Lord.[12]

- Priscilla and Aquila explained the way of God more perfectly to Apollos in their home in Ephesus.[13] The assembly in Ephesus also met in the home of Priscilla and Aquila, where we can only assume she had some very edifying things to say.[14]

- When males and females prophesy in a gathering, Paul says that "learning" is one of the outcomes.[15] Brothers and sisters are constantly learning more of Christ from one another. In this sense, it is clearly not wrong for women to contribute to the "learning" (*manthano*) of men.

1 Timothy 2:11-12

To gain a fuller understanding of verses 11 and 12, we must look at the text that precedes those verses:

> [8]I desire therefore that men pray everywhere, lifting up holy hands, without wrath and doubting. [9]In like manner also, that women adorn themselves in modest apparel, with decency and propriety; not with braided hair, or gold, or pearls, or costly array; [10]But (as becomes women professing godliness) with good works, [11]Let the woman learn in silence with all subjection. [12]But I permit not a woman to teach nor to have authority over the man, but to be in silence. (KJV2000)

The following observations from this passage would point away from it being a universal prohibition for all believing women, in all times and all cultures:

- Is there an imperative (command) in verse 11? No, it is a present tense verb: "I am not *allowing* a woman to teach…"

- Why does Paul move from plurals (men and women) to a singular (woman)? In verse 8, Paul wills that the men (plural) pray; in verses 9 and 10, he wills that when the women (plural) pray that they dress themselves in a certain way. But then in verses 11 and 12, Paul moved to the singular, "woman." Some have suggested that this indicates there was a problem—not with all the believing women in Ephesus—but with one (or a few). In light of this, it would seem very unlikely that the singular ("woman") should be used as a universal restriction on all sisters for all times. Paul was addressing a specific problem in Ephesus that is couched in singular, not plural language.

- Why is the Greek word *heseuchia* translated in some versions as "silence?" There is no basis for the concept of silence here. Paul used *heseuchia* in 1 Timothy 2:2, and there it means a "quiet" life. In 1 Timothy 2:11-12, *heseuchia* should also be translated as "quietness" (implying stillness, inner-tranquility, or God-produced calm). Because of problems connected with women coming out of a female-dominated religious cult, Paul saw that this woman should not be teaching in order to control a man, but should be learning in quietness. Quietness is not a trait connected just to females, but is to mark all believers as they walk through this evil age.[16] Men, women, and children all have to possess the demeanor of quietness in order to learn Christ from one another.

- How are the infinitives used in verse 12 to be correlated? Paul used two infinitives: "to teach" (*didaskein*) and "to control" (*authentein*). There are six options as to how these words could be correlated, but the best choice seems to be "purpose." That is, to teach with the goal of controlling another. It would be similar to our idioms, "hit-and-run," or "eat-and-run." Putting it in these terms, Paul would be saying, "teach-and-control." Women coming out of the Artemis cult could have easily had this problem. It is just as wrong for a man to teach with the goal of dominating others, and we know there has been plenty of that in church history!

In light of all the positive New Testament revelation about the freedom of women to function, I hope the above perspectives will help us see that it is improper to muzzle all women based on 1 Timothy 2:11-12. The New Testament is not against women teaching, but Paul does put the kibosh on a woman teaching with the goal of dominating a man, which was the specific problem in Ephesus.

1 Corinthians 14:33-36

[33] . . . for God is not a God of confusion, but of peace. As in all the churches of the saints, [34] let the women keep silence in the churches: for it is not permitted unto them to speak; but let them be in subjection, as also saith the law. [35] And if they would learn anything, let them ask their own husbands at home: for it is shameful for a woman to speak in the church. [36] What? was it from you that the word of God went forth? or came it unto you alone? (ASV)

There are some crucial perspectives to consider that demonstrate why it is a real stretch to use these verses to silence the sisters.

In "The Elusive Law," Cheryl Schatz presents evidence demonstrating that verses 34-35 are not Paul's words, but the remarks of some others in Corinth, based on the Talmud's restrictions on women.[17]

I've been wrestling with the issues raised regarding women in 1 Corinthians 11-14 for 31 years. For the first time, I feel as though significant light has broken through the lingering problems and questions. Without doubt, every conceivable explanation of what is entailed in 1 Corinthians 14:34-35 can be challenged from some angle. However, the position convincingly set forth by Schatz does the best job I've ever seen of doing justice to what the verses actually say in light of the immediate context, beginning in 1 Corinthians, chapter 11.

For a long time, I've wondered what "law" was in view in verse 34. There is strong reason to believe that it is not the Old Testament, but the rabbinic sayings that are being cited. These oral sayings were later put into writing. According to Wikisource: "The Talmud is a record of rabbinic discussions pertaining to Jewish law, ethics, customs, and history." In Jesus' day, the first part of the Talmud (the Mishnah) was in oral form. In 200 AD and 500 AD, it was put in writing. But even before Christ's life, the traditions of the elders had largely supplanted Moses as the principal source for conservative Jewish legal and spiritual interpretation. In other words, it was extra-biblical teaching created by an entrenched and politically motivated, religious, bureaucratic hierarchy.

In brief, two key issues point to why the Jewish oral law (Talmud) was behind what was stated in verses 34-35:

1. Only the Talmud silences women.

2. Only the Talmud designates the speech of women as "shameful."

Schatz observes, "The silencing of women was a Jewish ordinance. Women were not permitted to speak in the assembly or even to ask questions. The rabbis taught that a woman should know nothing but the use of her distaff."

Josephus, a Jewish historian, asserted that "the woman, says the law, is in all things inferior to a man. Let her accordingly be submissive."[18]

The Talmud clearly affirms the silence of females:

- "A woman's voice is prohibited because it is sexually provocative."[19]

- "Women are sexually seductive, mentally inferior, socially embarrassing, and spiritually separated from the law of Moses; therefore, let them be silent."[20]

The Talmud called the voice of a woman shameful:

- "It is a shame for a woman to let her voice be heard among men."[21]
- "The voice of a woman is filthy nakedness." [22]

When the Greek word, *aiskron,* is translated in English as "shameful" or "improper" in verse 35, it hardly conveys the strength of what the word encompasses. The affirmation, Schatz notes, is that a woman's speaking is "lewd, vile, filthy, indecent, foul, dirty, and morally degraded."

How could the same apostle who had just approved of women speaking, a few pen strokes later, turn around and unequivocally designate women's speech in the body as filthy, lewd, and vile? It makes no sense at all. I have always felt that verses 34-35 didn't sound like Paul. Something was awry.

The matter is greatly cleared up with the realization that Paul did not write the negative words about women in verses 34 and 35, but is quoting those who base their view of women on the oral law. Paul never required women to be silent and never called female speaking lewd and filthy. The Talmud was guilty of advocating both.

This is further confirmed in verse 36 when Paul exclaims, "What! Did the Word of God originate with you?" The "What!" indicates that Paul is not in harmony with what was stated by others from the Talmud in verses 34 and 35. Thayer's Lexicon notes that the "What!" is a disjunctive conjunction, which comes "before a sentence contrary to the one just preceding, to indicate that if one be denied or refuted, the other must stand."

Sir William Ramsey, a leading New Testament scholar, commented, "We should be ready to suspect that Paul is making a quotation from the letter addressed to him by the Corinthians whenever he alludes to their knowledge, or when any statement stands in marked contrast either with the immediate context or with Paul's known views."[23]

Those who use 1 Corinthians 14:34-35 as a basis for requiring the sisters to be silent in the meetings would do well to consider the strong possibility that the words they cite as proof-texts are completely non-Pauline; rather, they reflect the non-Gospel viewpoint of the Talmud. I submit that it is unthinkable that Paul would assign such awful sentiments as "dirty" and "like filthy nakedness" to the sisters' words.

In her book *Woman: God's Plan Not Man's Tradition*, Joanne Krupp points out:[24]

> The great German lexicographer, Schleusner, in his Greek-Latin Lexicon, declares that the expression 'as also saith the law' refers to the Oral Law of the Jews. Here are his words: 'The oral laws of the Jews or Jewish traditions...in the Old Testament no precept concerning the matter exists,' and he cites Vitringa as showing that it was 'forbidden by Jewish traditions for women to speak in the synagogue.'[25]

New Testament Women of Significance

I believe the information we have in the Bible about women participating in body life is extremely significant. Have you ever noticed that the New Testament offers many glimpses into the service of women in the Kingdom—more so than most of the original 12 apostles? In fact, the Lord gave us more information about the functioning of sisters in the early church than he did about a lot of other people, places, and matters in general.

Consider the following:

- Philip the Evangelist had four virgin daughters who prophesied.[26] There were probably many other women who had this gift too.

- Paul entrusted his letter to the Romans to Phoebe, and she delivered it. She was a deacon in the assembly at Cenchrea and Paul had the highest regard for her.[27] Paul recognized her as a prostatis, which carried with it the idea of leadership.[28]

- Paul designated Priscilla and Aquila as his "co-workers."[29] The same word is used with reference to people like Timothy and Titus.

- Paul greeted Junia and Andronicus (wife/husband or sister/brother) as "outstanding among the apostles."[30] They were his relatives and had been in prison with him. People (like Barnabas) were called "apostles" even though they were not among the Twelve. Junia was one of these apostolic workers. There is no reason to think that she was the only such female apostle.

- Among all the people Paul greeted in Romans 16, ten were sisters, among whom were "Tryphena and Tryphosa [who may have been twins], women who work hard for the Lord."[31]

- In line with Acts 2:17-18, Paul encouraged brothers and sisters to prophesy during gatherings.[32]

- The open meeting Paul described in 1 Corinthians 14 envisioned all the men and women (described as "the whole assembly" and "each one of you") functioning together in an encouraging manner, saying: "you may all prophesy one by one."

- Galatians 3:28 indicates that "in Christ," human distinctions, like male/female, are no longer norms of judgment. In the first century, prejudices abounded in folks' minds when certain labels like "Gentile," "Jew," "slave," and "woman" were mentioned. Paul said this should not be the case in the body of Christ.

- Women were prominent in the assembly at Philippi, beginning with Lydia's home. Paul asked for two sisters—who must have had no small spiritual influence in the body—to be at peace with one another.[33] He called Euodia and Syntyche "co-workers" and "co-strugglers" in the Gospel.

- Second John is addressed to "the elect lady and her children." This probably referred to a respected sister in whose home the saints gathered. She had apparently exerted significant spiritual influence upon a number of people. Women's homes were mentioned several times as meeting places for the brethren.[34]

- In Revelation 2:20-24, Christ rebuked the Thyatiran congregation for allowing a false prophetess, nicknamed "Jezebel," to "teach" some of the Lord's servants to sin grievously. If it was such a crime for a woman to teach the brethren, why didn't the Lord just condemn the assembly for even allowing a woman to instruct others? This incident in Thyatira implies that the assembly permitted other male and female prophets to teach the truth. Christ's bone to pick with them wasn't that a woman taught, but that *what* she taught was false teaching.

This survey concerning women is important because it reveals the freedom of the sisters to function in the Kingdom. In the general flow of the New Testament there are no restrictions on women.

Christ desires to express himself through both men and women. To restrict his expression to the male half of the priesthood is a slap in the face to the Lord—the One who died to create a new humanity where there was neither male nor female.

Discussion Questions

1. Have you ever been in a learning situation where women weren't allowed to speak or teach? Describe the experience. How did you feel?

2. What concept was most insightful to you in this chapter?

3. Women: What element of Jon's research was most affirming to you as a female follower of Jesus? How does this affect your confidence as a woman in ministry?

4. Men: How do Jon's insights affect your attitude toward women in the body of Christ?

5. Assuming Jon is correct in his interpretation of the challenging verses for women, what difference does this make?

Chapter 9 Notes

1. William Burkitt, Vicar and Lecturer of Dedham in Essex, *Expository Notes, with Practical Observations, on the New Testament of Our Lord & Saviour Jesus Christ, 4th Edition,* (London, 1709, loc. cit.).

2. Acts 2:17-18.

3. 1 Corinthians chapters 11 and 14.

4. John Piper, *What's the Difference? Manhood and Womanhood Defined According to the Bible,* (Wheaton: Crossway, 2008), 84.

5. Ephesians 4:20 (NKJV).

6. 2 Peter 3:18.

7. Colossians 3:16; Ephesians 5:19 (NKJV).

8. Hebrews 5:12.

9. Donald Joy, *Bonding: Relationships in the Image of God,* (Goshen: Evangel Publishing House, 1997), 25.

10. Jon Zens, *What's With Paul and Women? Unlocking the Cultural Background to 1 Timothy 2,* (Lincoln: Ekklesia Press, 2010).

11. Judges 2:16-19; 4:1-5:31.

12. 2 Kings 22:14-20; 2 Chronicles 34:22-28.

13. Acts 18:19-26.

14. 1 Corinthians 16:19.

15. 1 Corinthians 14:31.

16. 2 Thessalonians 3:12 (NKJV).

17. "Women in Ministry: Silenced or Set Free?," DVD #4, (Nelson, B.C.: MM Outreach, 2006).

18. *Contra Apioneum,* 2.201.

19. *Talmud, Berachot* 24a.

20. Summary of Talmudic sayings.

21. *Talmud, Tractate Kiddushin.*

22. *Talmud, Berachot Kiddushin.*

23. Sir William Mitchell Ramsey, *Historical Commentary on First Corinthians,* (Grand Rapids: Kregel Publications, 1996), 57.

24. Joanne Krupp, *Woman: God's Plan, Not Man's Tradition,* (Chelalis: Preparing the Way Publishers, 1999). 83.

25. Friedrich Schleusner, as quoted in Katherine Bushnell's, *God's Word to Women,* (privately reprinted [ca. 1976] by Ray B. Munson, [originally published, 1923]), 201.

26. Acts 21:9.

27. Romans 16:1-2.

28. Compare this to 1 Thessalonians 5:12.

29. Romans 16:3.

30. Romans 16:7.

31. Romans 16:12.

32. 1 Corinthians 11:4-5; 14:23-24.

33. Philippians 4:2-3.

34. Romans 16:5; 1 Corinthians 1:11; 1 Corinthians 16:19; Colossians 4:15.

LINDA BERGQUIST has been a catalytic church planter with Southern Baptists for 30 years. This relationship-based Kingdom servant is seasoned at training, mentoring, and coaching church planters, as well as interpreting cultures and creating strategy for all kinds of churches. She recognized her calling during a missions trip to an Arizona Apache reservation, just a few months after becoming a Christian. This large reservation needed a church, and Linda felt challenged to do something about it. This was her first baby step. She then planted two churches while attending a Southern Baptist seminary, and was subsequently called back to her home church to direct their missions program. Ten years and many churches later, Linda was offered a job in the San Francisco Bay Area helping the denomination start many more church plants. She also spearheaded a project (soaked in global prayer) called 10/10/10. The goal was to start 10 new churches on October 10, 2010. More than 40 churches were launched all over California! She has "discovered" church planters and midwifed church starts in mobile home parks, apartment complexes, master plan communities, and large churches—in both urban and suburban areas, including language-specific and multi-ethnic populations. Linda is widely respected among her peers for being fruitful to what God has clearly called her to. How can her example empower you for your destiny?

CHAPTER 10
A BOLD HERMENEUTIC

By Neil Cole

We love it when people force us to think outside the box. Neil Cole is neither traditional nor tame. He has a unique way of simplifying complicated topics by reducing them down to their basic principles directly from Scripture, challenging us to face the words and actions of Jesus. When he applies this perspective to leadership (a subject he has written about extensively[1]), we find ourselves grappling with unusual questions—ideas and principles that make sense but are definitely coloring outside the lines of traditional church thinking.

Neil, and the organization he works for, Church Multiplication Associates (CMA), trains church planters around the world in the principles of organic church—how to start churches in the harvest. Throughout the past decade, they have trained more than 45,000 people to multiply disciples, leaders, churches, and movements.

Enjoy having your thinking stretched in this chapter.

In a recent *Spiderman* blockbuster, a scientist fuses a lizard's DNA with his own in an attempt to regenerate a lost appendage. The result is a giant lizard-man that terrorizes Manhattan. Mutations create monsters.

Even though Jesus warned us not to, we have fused together two creatures to create a monster that has seized and held the church captive for centuries. We all suffer as a consequence. We took the beautiful bride of Christ and fused her DNA with an ugly monster found in the world system—one formed and led by the devil himself. The result is a mutation that has turned on us with fierce oppression.

Jesus' Word on Leadership is Primary

While addressing men who were striving to find their place in a hierarchical view of authority, Jesus spoke clearly and authoritatively about leadership that aspires for position in his Kingdom:

> You know that the rulers of the Gentiles lord it over them, and their great men exercise authority over them. It is not this way among you, but whoever wishes to become great among you shall be your servant...[2]

This statement is the baseline of revelation by which any other passage on leadership in God's Kingdom must be understood. It is primary when looking at New Testament leadership texts for the following four reasons:

1. The words are a direct and clear statement from our King addressing leadership in his Kingdom. He is the Head of the church. Neither Paul nor Peter would ever contradict Jesus.

2. The statement is repeated elsewhere in the Gospels and Christ also repeats the idea in other scenarios. Repetition is a strong way of emphasizing a point.

3. The statement is a clear and bold word that does not really allow for misinterpretation or misunderstanding.

   - People try to make this statement "safe" by saying the posture of a leader who is in a position of command should be that of a servant—"servant-leadership." But Jesus never told us to be servant leaders, he told us to be servants. Period. We would do far better with more servants and fewer leaders in the church.

   - Jesus' statement is not just about an attitude of the heart; it is about the way we are positioned in the Kingdom. He clearly states that we are not to be structured the way the world structures itself in regard to leadership. This is a direct assault on the hierarchical view of leadership.

4. It is consistent with the Gospel and the doctrines of the New Testament. As God's redeemed people, all of us are granted equal access, blessing, and empowerment in Christ's Kingdom. It does not violate the priesthood of all believers.

Using this passage as our basis dismantles some faulty views, and allows for a better hermeneutic (how a text is interpreted) regarding church leadership in general, and specifically as it relates to women. Our own cultural bias and religious traditions have skewed our understanding of leadership passages in the New Testament. A "bold hermeneutic" is willing to subject our traditions, dogma, and culture to the blaring light of Jesus' words.

The Cosmos

The world system, which the Scriptures refer to as the "cosmos," is designed as a hierarchical structure where an elite few are on top and the rest are somewhere under them in an oppressive pyramid of command and control. Value is derived from the service of another's vision. If you are not helping the leader (or leaders) on top succeed, you have less value. In this ugly system, some are considered better than others and intuitively have more rights and power.

Jesus clearly implied that this system is everywhere in the world. Indeed, we are all very familiar with it in the military, government, academia, business—even in crime.

Most cultures and societies are infused with this paradigm and people cannot imagine life without it. In a fallen world held captive by the prince of the power of the air, it's all we have.

The cosmos and the Kingdom are incompatible in every way, and we have mixed them to our own detriment. The Gospel of the Kingdom of Christ is counter-cultural.

Living Under a Curse

The hierarchy of men ruling over women takes root near the beginning of man's story, as shown in the Bible. In chapter 3 of Genesis, it is clearly presented as a direct result of the Fall, when sin entered the world through one man (Rom. 5:12). God tells Adam and Eve what's going to happen now that they know both good *and* evil—this is sometimes referred to as "the curse." Eve is told that she would have a desire for the man but that he would "rule over her." This is the failure of mankind, not the design of our Creator.

Speaking to the serpent first and then Eve, God says in Genesis 3:15-16:

'And I will put enmity between you and the woman, and between your seed and her seed; He shall bruise you on the head, and you shall bruise him on the heel' To the woman he said, 'I will greatly multiply your pain in childbirth. In pain you will bring forth children; yet your desire will be for your husband, and he will rule over you.'

Originally, women and men were to be one. In a redeemed Kingdom ruled by Christ's selfless love, that is the way it should be. In this Western Judeo-Christian world, the church has resisted this freedom and continued to establish boundaries and strongholds for a hierarchical worldview that puts women in a lower class, relegated to lesser influence.

This is perhaps our greatest shame. We are living as though Jesus' sacrifice was ineffective. Romans 5:17 shows that the curse has been undone:

For the sin of this one man, Adam, caused death to rule over many. But even greater is God's wonderful grace and his gift of righteousness, for all who receive it will live in triumph over sin and death through this one man, Jesus Christ.

Jesus died to break the curse. When we give in to a "curse worldview," we choose to live in the world system whose author is the "god of this world."

Unfortunately, there are aspects of the curse that we cannot escape in this fallen world. Even godly followers of Christ will have pain in childbirth, no matter how much they pray otherwise. Men have to work hard against the weeds and thorns of life because this is a universal consequence of a fallen world. We have no choice but to live in this world (that is passing away), but we do have a choice as to *how* we live.

The idea that men will rule over women is a relational consequence of the Fall, and of the enmity between the serpent and his offspring and the woman and her offspring. But we are given redemptive power to overcome this through the Gospel—foretold by God in the curse itself. We have a choice in how we relate to one another, because Christ's redemption (and our subsequent freedom) grants us that power.

Humanity's conflict with the serpent has a solution through a battle where both parties strike against the other. The enmity between the god of this world (the serpent of old) and the woman is redeemed. "Her Seed" (Christ) dealt a lethal blow to the head of the serpent who merely bruised his heel (on the cross).

The Gospel can overturn the relational consequence of the curse through Christ because it changes our very soul from within. We cannot overcome this consequence in the world as a whole, but within the Kingdom of Christ we both can and should. Christ became a curse (became sin) so that we do not have to endure that curse ourselves, to save us from the power of sin (Gal. 3:13, 2 Cor. 5:21, Rom. 6:7). Our relationships should be redeemed from the curse, not forever condemned to it.

Perhaps the church can influence the world with freedom and grace, just as she did with legalized slavery and in allowing women to vote. As Paul stated emphatically:

All of you are God's children because of your faith in Christ Jesus....Faith in Christ Jesus is what makes each of you equal with each other, whether you are a Jew or a Greek, a slave or a free person, a man or a woman. So if you belong to Christ, you are now part of Abraham's family, and you will be given what God has promised.[3]

The cosmos is the way of the fallen world and the design of the god of this world. We have allowed this worldly and ungodly command and control system to infiltrate and dominate the church. The result is a monster that carries out the oppression of the world system with religious fervor and devotion. This monster legitimizes itself with the counterfeit stamp of God's authority as a mandate to function in an illegitimate way. We have allowed the same serpent into our garden again and he is still telling us the same old lies. The monster must be stopped.

A Better Authority

In the cosmos, there is delegated authority from a top-down chain of command. In the Kingdom, there is distributed authority based upon each person's direct connection to the King himself—Jesus.

We are not to be patterned after the world; we are to be a body of Christ, a Kingdom of God where there is neither male nor female, slave nor free. We must stimulate a new imagination of what can be, or we will forever be subject to what is. Imagine a Kingdom ruled by Jesus, where each of us has direct contact with the King and moves at his impulse. Imagine what a loving and all-knowing Creator could do with a body so responsive to his voice.

Positional authority is a weak authority. It is unnecessary in the Kingdom of God where we can exercise relational and spiritual authority based on Christ's rule and reign. When James and John were seeking positional authority, to "exercise authority over" others, Jesus emphatically said, "It is not to be so among you."[4]

Everywhere in the New Testament where leadership is addressed, spiritual character is the basis of authority—not position, talent, or gender. In a body where authority is proven by character, position is unnecessary and counterproductive. Character is not a means to gain positional authority; it is the only authority needed. Christ in us is our basis of authority. The longer we walk in his Spirit, the more his authority is evident in our lives. Jesus didn't die and rise from the dead to give his authority (that comes from a godly life) to half the church. His life is available to all of us—men and women alike.

The whole debate about women in church ministry is predicated upon a cosmos worldview and grounded in a curse, not a biblical ideal. Think about it. We place women in a less-authoritative place in the chain of command, where their position is more limited. This is a cosmos worldview and "it is not to be so among you."

The solution is clear. It doesn't help to place women higher up the chain of command; we need to eliminate the pyramid altogether. Once positional authority is devalued in the Kingdom, the debate about where women (or minorities, or children) fit in the pecking order is irrelevant. Once every person is seen as a redeemed agent of God's Kingdom, under the direct command of Christ—the rightful and true King—all debate is over.

Leadership Untainted by the Cosmos

If we remove the cosmos-worldview lenses from the New Testament, we see some dramatic changes in how we are to relate to God, one another, and the world. Alternatives to the typical cosmos view of New Testament passages on leadership, and specifically women in leadership, can be reconciled without imposing a faulty hierarchical dogma on them.

ELDERS: People often automatically presume that because elders are appointed in the church, a hierarchy exists there. Is it possible to appoint elders and not violate Jesus' command regarding authority and hierarchy found in the Gospels?

We needn't see a hierarchy simply because we recognize elders. There is a very consistent usage of prepositions in the New Testament passages related to leadership that contrasts with what is common in the world. Not only did Jesus use these prepositions, but Peter also repeated the pattern. Jesus contrasted those who are "over" with true servants being "among."

1 Peter 5:1-3 (NASB) says (prepositions underlined):

> Therefore, I exhort the elders <u>among</u> you, as your fellow elder and witness of the sufferings of Christ. . . shepherd the flock of God <u>among</u> you, exercising oversight not under compulsion, but voluntarily, according to the will of God; and not for sordid gain, but with eagerness; nor yet as lording it <u>over</u> those allotted to your charge, but proving to be examples to the flock.

To equate leadership with offices and positions is a grave mistake in melding the cosmos with the Kingdom. Elders can influence others without needing a position or title—hard to imagine given our immersion for so long in the cosmos, but nevertheless possible.

Church leaders and scholars throw around the term "office" when referring to leadership in the church. A cursory read of many Bible translations finds the term office in 1 Timothy 3:1, but the word was not originally in any part of the New Testament. Bible translators, lacking the imagination to understand a Kingdom without an institutional hierarchy, thought Paul needed their help explaining leadership to the common Christian. But they taught something Paul did not.

I see an elder functioning in a spiritual family like a father or mentor to those in the family. They are to model and lead by example among the people.[5] Oversight is not looking down, but looking over the flock to watch for incoming threats and prepare for any potential danger. A father has a natural authority in a family based upon who he is, but if his character is lacking, he might resort to positional authority—"Because I said so!" This is why the role of elder is based upon sound and proven character, not a job description or spiritual gift. Fruit of the Spirit is where our authority is found, not the gifts of the Spirit.

Jesus had no title or position during his day, "for he was teaching them as one having authority, and not as their scribes."[6] He had a better authority, one not dependent upon a place in the chain of command. If you need a position to get your job done, then you are not qualified for the position. If you can get your job done without position, why would you want or need a position?

In addition to elders, are there other roles that provide leadership? Yes. Apostles, prophets, evangelists, shepherds, and teachers are given to the church to equip her for the work of ministry.[7] Again, the natural authority for these roles comes from mature character—it is not based on the gifts themselves, nor on gender (positional authority).

DEACONS: Is a deacon or deaconess simply a junior varsity elder who does the unglamorous work so the elders don't have to? Do they simply count the offering, hand out bulletins, and clean up after the potluck? Why do we assume an elder is at the top of the "chain of command"?

Many are quick to point out that the difference in qualification between an elder and a deacon is the ability to teach. Does that establish the deacon as a second-tier servant who does not actually lead? I think not. Because we have turned church into a teaching center, the leader who teaches is viewed above others, but this is definitely not what the Bible prescribes. There could very well be other reasons why an ability to teach is not listed under the qualities of a deacon or deaconess.

I believe it is entirely possible that the role of deacon/deaconess is a mature expression of the equipping gifts mentioned in Ephesians 4:11. Could it be that deacons and deaconesses are actually apostles, prophets, evangelists, shepherds, and teachers that equip the saints for the work of ministry? I suggest it is an interpretation more worthy of our consideration than the more traditional view for the following reasons:

1. The descriptions listed for elders and deacons are equally high. Both are to help lead the family or household of God.[8] Perhaps the ability to teach mentioned for elders is not to separate that role as higher, but rather as a minimum for influence within a more contained context. An elder is more focused on a specific spiritual family (what we would see as a missional community or organic church today), so the expression of their task is more defined. In contrast, perhaps a deacon or deaconess serves on a broader scale and is capable of many ministry assignments, which may or may not include "teacher." For instance, someone may be a deaconess who doesn't serve as a teacher, but instead as a prophetess or a shepherd. To say that person must be a teacher (or nothing at all) would violate the diversity of these gifts and the effects of their influence.

2. When settling a debate among the disciples about who was on top of the pyramid, Jesus didn't say it was a teacher, elder, or leader. He clearly said that the greatest in the Kingdom is a deacon—a servant. The word "deacon" comes from the Greek *diakonos*. This very same word is translated as "servant" in Jesus' important statement regarding a non-hierarchical viewpoint of leadership: "...whoever wishes to become great among you shall be your servant (*diakonos*)."[9]

I am not suggesting that deacons are higher in the chain of command. We are all to be servants. I contend that some who have matured and been tested as servants over time will emerge to serve in a more formal function as deacons. These people, because of their tested experience, will "equip the saints to do the work of ministry," which is serving our Head. (The root word for deacon is used in this instance too, translated here as ministry.)[10]

While an elder must be "able to teach,"[11] it is said that the deacon and deaconess must "first be tested," and then they can serve in the role. This may be a more stringent qualification than simply being "apt to teach."

Are all elders also deacons? To parent a small group of Christ-followers that functions like a family does not require the level of maturity and experience that equipping the saints for ministry requires. Serving as a deacon or deaconess is not in any way inferior to serving as an elder; they are simply different roles in differing contexts.

3. In the early church, a complaint arose because care for the widows of Hellenistic Jews was being neglected. Rather than put more work on the current apostles, the church appointed what many believe to be the first deacons.[12] Their task was to "serve" (again, the Greek word that was used in this instance is the same root word used for deacon). They were Spirit-filled and of great character. However, they didn't limit their activities to waiting on tables. They boldly preached the Gospel—prophesying, performing miracles, and doing cross-cultural church planting.[13] One of them was actually given another description—Philip is called "the evangelist,"[14] one of the very roles mentioned in Ephesians 4:11.

4. Even in the early church, apostles seemed on equal footing with the elders in Jerusalem. The decree accepting Gentiles as members of the church without having to become Jewish came from James and the elders, as well as Peter and the apostles. Neither is seen above or below the other.[15] Could this be the elders and deacons reasoning together with the Holy Spirit?

In the New Testament, the deacon role is not limited to men,[16] though it carries the qualification of being a "husband of one wife," as does the role of elder.[17] The meaning of this expression, which literally translates as "a one-woman man," is that someone is devoted for life to one spouse. There are both deacons and deaconesses[18] in the New Testament and both should be devoted husbands and wives. Perhaps this is also true of elders.

PASTORS: There is one role that gets all the attention in the church today: pastor. The corresponding Greek word, *poimen,* which means "shepherd" or "pastor," is used four times in the New Testament in reference to Christ,[19] but only once to describe a church leader other than Jesus.[20] Of the five roles in Ephesians 4:11, pastor is the least used title in the New Testament but the most used in the church. Why are we so quick to call someone pastor, even though this happens only once in the Bible?

This role has become the catch-all for church leadership and has been reserved almost exclusively for men. There is no biblical precedence for excluding women from this role—the single appearance of pastor in the New Testament (as related to church functions) does not specify gender. In fact, the context of Ephesians is the entire universal body of Christ, not just the half with a Y chromosome.

Shepherding is in fact a role that may be better suited for women in many instances. There are several times that a pastoral response is presented in the Bible using a female example. Jesus spoke of a mother hen gathering her chicks together.[21] Paul uses a mother's example in how he responded in pastoral care toward the Thessalonians saying:

> But we proved to be gentle among you, as a nursing mother tenderly cares for her own children. Having so fond an affection for you, we were well-pleased to impart to you not only the gospel of God but also our own lives, because you had become very dear to us.[22]

It is irresponsible to restrict pastoral care to only the male half of the church, when there is likely a lot more nurturing care on the maternal side of the aisle.

OTHER LEADERSHIP ROLES: We also find a woman apostle named Junia in the New Testament.[23] Paul honors her by calling her "outstanding among the apostles." There have been several futile attempts to change her name to a masculine form in order to reinforce a faulty cosmos view of leadership. Any sound New Testament scholar today will confirm that this name is clearly feminine.

Several times, women are called prophets in the New Testament.[24] It is explicitly stated that they will prophesy.[25] Women are also instructed to teach. In addition to the general exhortations meant for all Christians,[26] women specifically are to "teach what is good."[27]

Church Practices

How about baptism? Many are quick to say that women should neither teach nor baptize. But is this truly what the whole of the Bible tells us? Jesus said:

> I have been given all authority in heaven and on earth. Therefore, go and make disciples of all the nations, baptizing them in the name of the Father and the Son and the Holy Spirit. Teach these new disciples to obey all the commands I have given you. And be sure of this: I am with you always, even to the end of the age.[28]

This passage is directed to all disciples of all nations to the end of the age—not just the 12 apostles, and certainly not to men alone. The world needs the whole body of Christ to fulfill the Great Commission, not just the male half. When all authority of heaven and earth commands that women baptize and teach, the question should be settled.

The idea that only clergy should practice baptism and communion is foreign to the New Testament. The opposite is actually found. Jesus let his disciples baptize for him.[29] Paul says to the Corinthians that he was glad he only baptized a few.[30] When Paul arrived in Corinth, he was alone. If he didn't baptize more people who did? The newly baptized!

A False Dichotomy

Theologians have a habit of designing a false dichotomy with two sides that are not necessarily opposites, then presenting a false choice of one or the other. In the issue of women in leadership roles, theologians have presented us with this choice:

1. A complementarian position where women and men are different and therefore fulfill different roles in the Kingdom

2. An egalitarian view where both men and women are viewed as equal in all things

The problem with this proposition is that these two sides are not actually in conflict. I believe they are both correct, not on opposite ends of a spectrum. I am a complementary egalitarian. Men and women are different and equal. Why do we feel the need to put one above another? Perhaps we have let the cosmos infiltrate our worldview and influence our relationships. The truth is that women and men are equal in importance, significance, and giftedness. Let's not flush away the beautiful uniqueness that is in women, but let's not subordinate them in an oppressive cosmos view of church structure either.

Hermeneutics

A bold hermeneutic is needed. Most proclaim the need for a solid hermeneutic. What they mean too often is a conservative system that confirms their unchanging and very outdated doctrinal bias. A hermeneutic that arrives at a conclusion contrary to their point of view is then labeled a poor hermeneutic.

We need a hermeneutic that allows the Bible to speak for itself rather than us using it to verify our already established beliefs. Are we able to accept a scriptural idea even if it costs us our cherished theology and ancient traditions? Can we do that even if we've inherited hundreds of years of dogma that is suddenly found contrary to Scripture? Are we to accept Scripture, even at the cost of our denominational structure? This is what I mean by a bold hermeneutic.

Jesus said we only serve one master. We cannot incorporate the cosmos and the Kingdom into the church in a healthy way. We must choose one or the other. When we try to marry the two, we create a monster that wreaks havoc on lives. We cannot serve God and the cosmos.

This chapter was adapted from Neil's book, Primal Fire. *(Tyndale House Publishers, 2014)*

Discussion Questions

1. How has the cosmos influenced your view of leadership?

2. What were your presuppositions about elders and deacons before you read this chapter? Have they changed?

3. Do you believe women should be ordained? Why or why not?

4. What affect will this chapter have on your leadership style? When and how will you implement this?

Chapter 10 Notes

1. Neil Cole, *Organic Leadership: Leading Naturally Right Where You Are,* (Ada: Baker Books, 2010); *Journeys to Significance: Charting a Leadership Course from the Life of Paul,* (Hoboken: Jossey Bass, 2011).

2. Mark 10:41-43 (NASB).

3. Galatians 3:26-29 (CEV).

4. Matthew 20:26.

5. 1 Peter 5:3 (NASB).

6. Matthew 7:29; Mark 1:22; Luke 4:32.

7. Ephesians 4:11-12.

8. 1 Timothy 3:12. Under the elder's description (a better word than "qualification"), it says the reason for them leading their own household well relates to leading in the church assembly. So when deacons are described the same way, the idea would naturally be consistent.

9. Matthew 20:26.

10. Ephesians 4:11-12.

11. 1 Timothy 3:2.

12. Acts 6:1-6.

13. Acts 6-8.

14. Acts 21:8.

15. Acts 15.

16. 1 Timothy 3:8-13.

17. 1 Timothy 3:2, 12.

18. Romans 16:1; 1 Timothy 3:8-13.

19. John 10:11, 14; Hebrews 13:20; 1 Peter 2:25.

20. Ephesians 4:11. The cognate verb of *poime,* "to shepherd or tend a flock," is used in Acts 20:28 and 1 Peter 5:1-4 to describe the function of leaders. It is also used by Jesus in John 21:16 to describe what Peter should do in the church. Even still, that is very few references, compared to, say, descriptions of the apostolic or prophetic roles.

21. Matthew 23:37.

22. 1 Thessalonians 2:7-8 (NASB).

23. Romans 16:7.

24. Luke 2:36; Acts 21:9.

25. Acts 2:17-18.

26. Matthew 28:19-20; 1 Corinthians 14:26; Colossians 3:16; Hebrews 5:12.

27. Titus 2:3.

28. Matthew 28:18-20.

29. John 4:2.

30. 1 Corinthians 1:13-17.

PART FOUR

JUSTICE FOR WOMEN

RESCUE HER is a non-profit charity that fights human trafficking. It was founded by Josie Carignan, a wife and young mother of three. Josie was born with a desire to help the helpless in the darkest of places. She asked herself, "What could one person possibly do to make a difference?" In 2009, God spoke to her heart saying: "My light is greater than even this darkness. And it is okay that you can't help everybody, but you *can* rescue one…and then another, and another." Out of that moment, Rescue Her was born. God helped Josie think beyond being an at-home mom in a small town with little access to startup money. A lot of creativity and hard work followed. Today, tiny steps of faith still matter. Rescue Her now sponsors safe houses for underage victims of sex trafficking in Cambodia and India. They offer counseling, education, vocational training, and when possible, family reconciliation. The ministry reaches out to teen girls who are at high risk of being trafficked and is fueled by prayer networks all over the world. Rescue Her also offers internships to others wanting to make a difference. It is amazing to see all that the Lord has done through Josie and the Rescue Her team in the last three years. Sometimes all it takes is asking God the right question.

CHAPTER 11

JUSTICE FOR DAUGHTERS OF A KING

By Julie Ross

The team of women involved in writing this book is not comprised of angry feminists. Nor are we nursing hurts from the past. Rather, we have a passion to see justice for women. Ever since the Fall, women have been oppressed—probably more than any other segment of society, they have been abused, neglected, mistreated, and enslaved. From the very start of his ministry, Jesus declared an open war on injustice: he had come to bring good news to the poor, to comfort the brokenhearted, to proclaim liberty to the captives, to set at liberty those who are oppressed. The church should embody this mission of Jesus.

Julie Ross is an example of a disciple that's on mission. She served at a US YWAM base as a trainer and director of HomeFront (a training preparation and pastoral care team serving dozens of church planters). She wrote and produced national advocacy radio initiatives on the needs of women and children in 10/40 window countries (the area between 10 degrees north and 40 degrees north latitude, which has little access to the Christian message). She writes from her extensive experience in other nations—30 ministry trips into a dozen nations on three continents—about the injustice toward women she has witnessed around the world.

How bad is it…really? Consider this custom of the Guarani, an indigenous people group in Paraguay. When a woman has a baby, it's the man who takes a rest. He takes several days to "rest his seed," while the woman gets right back to work. When I learned this, I didn't know whether to laugh or cry.

Justice is a concept based on truth and established legitimacy. Justice cries out for what "ought to be." There's no question that the female gender has been at the crosshairs of human history on almost every front. The book, *Why Not Women,*[1] by Loren Cunningham and David Hamilton offers powerful insight into realities for those simply born...female. "No gender has been more aborted, abused, exploited, humiliated, persecuted, murdered, and enslaved. From this generation alone, between 60 and one hundred million girls are missing—killed by their families because of their gender."[2] Other sources indicate that even this heartbreaking estimate may be conservative.

Husband and wife team Nicholas Kristof and Sheryl WuDunn authored a stunning book in 2010 called *Half the Sky*[3] (which was adapted into a PBS series and a movie). It highlights stark and stubborn gender-equality obstacles in the nations and solutions manifested by those who care enough to make a difference. Often it's the victims of injustice themselves who garner the resolve to say, "enough is enough" and partner with grassroots activists.

Does a robust view of biblical justice encompass justice for all? Here's a thumbnail sketch of the real female drama that is playing out globally as we speak:

- Other than drug dealing, human trafficking is tied with the illegal arms industry as the second-largest criminal industry in the world today, and it is the fastest growing. According to US Government–sponsored research completed in 2006, approximately 800,000 people are trafficked across national borders annually; this estimate does not include the millions trafficked within their own countries. Ninety-eight percent of sex-trafficking victims are women and girls.[4]

- Mass rapes occur at mind-boggling levels. A UN report claims that 90 percent of girls and women over the age of three were sexually abused in parts of Liberia during the civil war. Sexual violence in Congo is the worst in the world, according to John Holmes, UN Undersecretary General for Humanitarian Affairs. In 2008, the UN formally declared rape as a "weapon of war."[5] In

Pakistan, "honor rapes" result from an obsession with virginity, and the authorities are indifferent to injustice suffered by the poor and uneducated.[6]

- Worldwide, poverty has a female face.

- Child marriage stunts any chance at a normal future for millions of girls.

- Gendercide, the systematic killing of members of a certain sex, occurs in horrific numbers. "In parts of Asia—especially India and China—baby girls are undesirable, even unacceptable."[7] Millions have been aborted, discarded, or drowned due to the one-child policy in China that strongly prefers boys.

- Seven hundred and eighty million people in the world are illiterate; two-thirds of these are girls and women.[8]

- According to Nobel Prize Committee Chairman, Thorbjorn Jagland, the oppression of women is the single most important issue in the Arab world.[9] In 2004, Grand Mufti Sheik Abdul-Aziz of Saudi Arabia said, "Allowing women to mix with men is the root of every evil and catastrophe. It is highly punishable."[10]

It takes your breath away, doesn't it?

Gender Justice in the Nations

I had an interesting conversation in my home not long ago with a man from Saudi Arabia who is a Wahabi Muslim. In his country, women must obtain permission from their guardian—usually a father or husband—to work, travel, study, or marry; and in divorce, the man gets custody of the children. Saudi Arabia is the only country in the world that prohibits women from driving a car.

Manal al Sharif, a woman who bucked the system and did drive, was a hot topic in the news. During our conversation, my friend, who is quite enlightened to Western ways, still reflected, "Women want to drive. But why?" Manal, who was incarcerated for nine days for simply driving a car, now helps to spearhead a national movement in her country. In December 2012, a member of the Consultative Assembly (the formal advisory board to the King of Saudi Arabia) submitted a report to the Assembly that said lifting the driving ban would cause prostitution, pornography, homosexuality, divorce, and the "end of virginity"—but he was open for more dialogue.[11] On a brighter note, King Abdullah decreed that women would be allowed to vote in municipal elections starting in 2015.

Traveling in the developing nations presents many opportunities to take note of gender injustice. One of the cultural norms in Kyrgyzstan, especially in villages, is called "bride stealing." A man observes and chooses who he wants to marry, then he and his pals chase down the girl, he rapes her, and she is culturally obliged to marry him. It's considered shameful for her family to consider taking her back. A darling, young, female friend of mine in Kyrgyzstan routinely practiced running to prepare for this season in her life, firmly planning to outrun anyone with this intention. She succeeded, and eventually married a believer.

Our team there shared heartrending accounts of helping young women who came to them fearful and at risk. Their success was mixed. Even as some of these young women are "forced" to marry, our team does what it can to stay in the loop and nourish both the woman and her newly gained husband. As the Scripture says: "Do not be overcome by evil but overcome evil with good."[12]

I once paid a pastoral visit to an American missionary family living in a relatively remote area of Uzbekistan. Among other things, they hosted an English language club for young women. The young women expressed curiosity about American weddings. The family prayed and came up with a creative idea. They made copies of the following typical "wedding" verses for the students, both in English and Uzbek:

> Love is patient and kind. Love is not jealous or boastful or proud or rude. Love does not demand its own way. Love is not irritable, and it keeps no record of when it has been wronged. It is never glad about injustice, but rejoices whenever the truth wins out. Love never gives up, never loses faith, is always hopeful, and endures through every circumstance.[13]

These young women were astonished. They had never heard anything like this, but immediately recognized it as truth. Some even memorized the verses. They expressed strong emotions and deep longing at the concept of love actually being a part of marriage.

On another occasion, when traveling to Afghanistan, I had the privilege of meeting a few times with a particular Afghan woman who shares her husband with other wives. No, it is most certainly not something she wanted or enjoys, but her very survival depends on staying connected to a man. While I couldn't help her personal situation, I could sit with her, listen to her heart, pray with her, and care. We exchanged small gifts as reminders of our friendship.

I learned of a mullah (a Muslim cleric) in a poor village in Afghanistan who, by God's grace, became a Christian believer. He had two wives. When he was made aware of the biblical reference to be the "husband of one wife," his personal response was to withhold food from one of his wives so that she starved to death!

I was welcomed to visit a very poor and isolated Afghan village that had no viable roads, medical care, or schools. Ignorance is almost always the enemy; education is almost always a golden key. Much earlier, our team had inquired in this village to see if the men had any interest in learning to read Dari, their native Afghan language. The general response was, "What a waste of time that would be; we are way too busy." Then the question was posed, "Well, if you are too busy, could we teach your women to read?" Their answer was basically, "The women are stupid, but you can try if you want to."

Our missions team developed some rudimentary primary readers (all educational materials had, by that time, been destroyed by the Taliban), and hired several Dari-literate women from a neighboring region to teach. A pioneer-minded auntie from the village was one of the first to become literate and began hosting a handful of women in her home for Dari lessons.

As an incentive to get the ball rolling, US churches had assembled zip-sack packets that included soap, combs, washrags, and small stuffed animals, which were offered as incentives to the ladies if they completed three months of regular language lessons. After the first three months, some of these ladies had a great idea. If they were willing to attend another three months of lessons, could they get another packet to give to a relative? Sure! Long story short, literacy was multiplying. Women were learning to read and write in their own language. (This opens up worlds of opportunity for growth, development, the ability to enter the world of commerce, etc.) Sometime later, when the prospect of building a school came up, guess who proposed that girls should be allowed to attend? The mothers from the language classes! Their success in learning to read and write fostered a hunger within for the same opportunity for their eager daughters.

For a number of years, I have been privileged to serve on the board of directors of a ministry called Mission Impact.[14] I have trained staff and taken many US teams to serve in a remote area of Guatemala. In rural Guatemala, if girls are educated at all, it's generally only until third grade. After that, they typically tend the home, make tortillas, oversee younger siblings by carrying them on their backs, and the like. Pursuing an actual vocation is usually out of reach. Eleven years ago, one of our teams started a grade school targeting the most unprivileged girls in an indigenous Mayan village. To give you a sense of the culture, some of these girls have never even touched a car, much less ridden in one. This year we are educating 120 girls in grades one through six. In addition to an education, they get weekly showers, lice checks, home visits to engage parents in their education, Bible study, and vocational training in baking, sewing, and other useful skills. This is a practical "justice response" to a beautiful culture that inadvertently devalues females.

In 2000, the President of Western Sahara, Mohamed Abdelaziz, invited Window International Network and its co-founder, Beverly Pegues, to form a needs-assessment team to journey to one of the five Sahrawi (Western Sahara) refugee camps situated in the harsh Algerian Sahara desert. I had the unusual opportunity join them.

Here's the backstory: Morocco coveted Western Sahara's rich natural resources. In 1975, Morocco's military invaded Western Sahara and a 16-year war ensued. Half of Western Sahara's population was forced into the desert with napalm, killing many men, women, and children. The Sahara Desert is incredibly inhospitable. There are no trees to speak of and temperatures rise to 130 degrees during the day. Imagine being one of the 90,000 Sahrawi (UN estimate) living in a hostile natural environment in a refugee camp for 38 years and counting. At the time of our visit in 2000, the Sahrawi refugees had been living in tents for a quarter-century, and all fresh water, firewood, and food had to be hauled in.

Women have played a strategic role in camp administration, especially during the war. All leaders of the districts (neighborhood organizations) in the camps are women. In fact, this is a proud example in the Arab world of a people who genuinely support women's equality.

Among other accomplishments amid difficult conditions, they developed their own educational system, and are considered to be the most literate people in Africa. The Sahrawi women are gifted weavers. I watched their rhythmic weaving at large looms, and noticed they had to use rough, cotton string for their delicate creations. Several pairs of scissors were shared by all the women of the camp. Kept under lock and key, these scissors were brought out for us to see. Some of the women pointed to the tips of their fingers, rubbed them, and conveyed a sad countenance. They were demonstrating a simple need for thimbles to protect their fingers while sewing.

When I returned to the US, I garnered the support of my home church to donate dozens of sewing tools for the women and soccer balls for the kids, among other helpful items. It took some unusual logistics, but we arranged to have them couriered into the camps. We didn't save the world, but we helped make a difference.

In Asuncion, Paraguay, there's a large women's prison called Buen Pastor (translated "good pastor"). I was there with a team, invited by the wife of the country's president. She was aware of the poor prison conditions and was encouraging solutions to help the inmates. Prison ministry had started just a year prior for the ladies, and volunteers were being trained. When I was there, more than two-thirds of the women were awaiting a formal hearing—some, after several months in prison. Many of the women were victims of domestic violence. In Paraguay, the men do not spend time behind bars for domestic violence but the women do, typically because they try to defend themselves.

Spending time and praying with Lucia, a prisoner from Argentina, was a highlight. She was the daughter of Argentine missionaries to Holland but rebelled for a season, left home, and landed in Paraguay where she lived with a man she didn't know well—she didn't even know he owned a gun. The police came to the door one morning to arrest him for murder, and she was promptly arrested as an accessory to his crime. When I met her, she had already been incarcerated at Buen Pastor for six months, without so much as having been formally accused of anything, while her boyfriend had long ago been released from prison. She was serving as a worship leader inside the prison, trusting God for her eventual release.

> A bruised reed he will not break—and a smoldering (dimly burning) wick he will not quench, until he brings justice and a just cause to victory.[15]

The Fragrance of Justice in the US

One of the Lord's biblical mandates to us is to "…do justice, love mercy, and walk humbly with thy God."[16]

Jimmy Carter was president of the US from 1977 to 1981. After 60 years in the Southern Baptist Church, he made a strong statement with his decision to leave as a result of its limiting stance on women in ministry. In his public position paper, he stated:

> It is simply self-defeating for any community to discriminate against half its population. We need to challenge these self-serving and outdated attitudes and practices.... At its most repugnant, the belief that women must be subjugated to the wishes of men excuses slavery, violence, forced prostitution, genital mutilation, and national laws that omit rape as a crime. But it also costs many millions of girls and women control over their own bodies and lives, and continues to deny them fair access to education, health, employment, and influence within their own communities.

> This view that women are somehow inferior to men is not restricted to one religion or belief. Women are prevented from playing a full and equal role in many faiths. Nor, tragically, does its influence stop at the walls of the church, mosque, synagogue, or temple. This discrimination, unjustifiably attributed to a Higher Authority, has provided a reason or excuse for the deprivation of women's equal rights across the world for centuries.... I understand, however, why many political leaders can be reluctant about stepping into this minefield. Religion and tradition are powerful and sensitive areas to challenge. But my fellow elders and I, who come from many faiths and backgrounds, no

longer need to worry about winning votes or avoiding controversy—and we are deeply committed to challenging injustice wherever we see it.

The same discriminatory thinking lies behind the continuing gender gap in pay and why there are still so few women in office in the West. The root of this prejudice lies deep in our histories, but its impact is felt every day. It is not women and girls alone who suffer. It damages all of us. The evidence shows that investing in women and girls delivers major benefits for society.[17]

In the US, gender injustice isn't typically fraught with banal brutality, but it is no less part and parcel of the fabric of our culture. According to *USA Today* reporter Christina Dugas, "We have equal-pay laws that have been on the books for a very long time, but we still have unequal pay, which suggests a need for stronger enforcement or new legislation."[18] The way things are is not the way they ought to be.

Carly Fiorina, former CEO of Hewlett-Packard, has pointed out the solid merits of having women's input at the board of director level. But the reality is, even in our enlightened Western culture, only 3 percent of board members in the US are female.[19] Many men concede they simply don't have experience working with women. Interestingly, it's been shown that whenever a man has a positive experience working with a woman, barriers come down. Whenever women are not held back by prejudice, bias, and stereotyping, barriers give way and justice prevails. In many European countries, women have long had rights and privileges alongside men. It's curious that the USA lags so far behind by comparison.

God's Delight

Psalm 37:28 says that God delights in justice. When God said it wasn't good for man to be alone, that was a blanket statement— not just about marriage, but about his vision for humanity. Both genders are called by God to come alongside him in this battle. We are supposed to be in this battle together.

I have tromped around many countries with principled and compassionate men, working side by side, blending our gifts and callings. I am honored to call them friends and Kingdom co-laborers.

We "do justice" when we befriend victims, seed and feed hope, protect others from harm, advocate, adopt, give, and support those who go out to minister. We practice justice when we intercede, and when we introduce people to Jesus. As we, the body of Christ, become more proficient in honoring and calling forth each other's gifts and talents, we learn how to work better together and network beyond our personal spheres of influence. We can petition, run for office, pass legislation, make movies, and target whole villages for transformation.

How has God deposited compassion in you? What injustice or justice are you passionate about? Are your eyes on your long personal list of limitations or on who you are in him? Is your church or fellowship postured to walk the walk?

If you are a serious "image bearer" of Christ, you have, by definition, made yourself available to "bear witness" to truth. Justice is rooted in eternal truth. Best-selling author and activist Shane Claiborne defines living as salt and light in two words: truth bearing. Here's the warning—it will cost us. At the very least, our convictions should inconvenience us from time to time. History is laced with those who have gone as far as to lay down their life for another.[20] Jesus gave his life for all of us. The prophet Amos admonishes us to let justice run down like waters and righteousness flow like a mighty ever-flowing stream.[21]

Let's do that.

Discussion Questions

1. Do you think it is important to care about or educate yourselves on the challenges women face in other parts of the world? Why or why not?

2. What international injustice issue regarding girls/women do you consider to be most serious?

3. Have you ever taken any kind of action on behalf of justice for women? What prompted you to do so? What happened?

4. What are you going to do as a result of reading this chapter?

Chapter 11 Notes

1. Loren Cunningham and Joel David Hamilton, *Why Not Women: A Biblical Study of Women in Missions, Ministry, and Leadership*, (Seattle: YWAM Publishing, 2000).

2. Ibid, 20.

3. Nicholas D. Kristof and Sheryl WuDunn, *Half the Sky: Turning Oppression into Opportunity for Women Worldwide*, (New York: Vintage, 2010).

4. US Department of State, "Trafficking in Persons Report 2012," accessed December 2013, http://www.state.gov/j/tip/rls/tiprpt/2012/index.htm.

5. Kristof and WuDunn, *Half the Sky*, 84.

6. Ibid, 83.

7. "200 Million Girls Killed in China, Where Are the Feminists?" LifeNews.com, November 2012, http://www.lifenews.com/2012/11/02/200-million-girls-killed-in-china-where-are-the-feminists.

8. John Wood, Room to Read initiative.

9. *Associated Press News*, 10/7/2011.

10. *New York Times* article, 1/22/2004.

11. Sebastian Usher, *BBC News*, 12/2/2011.

12. Romans 12:21(NIV).

13. 1 Corinthians 13:4-7.

14. http://www.missionimpact.com/, accessed December 2013.

15. Matthew 12:20 (AMP).

16. Micah 6:8 (NASB).

17. Jimmy Carter, "Losing my religion for equality," *The Age*, July 2009, http://www.theage.com.au/opinion/losing-my-religion-for-equality-20090714-dk0v.html#ixzz2MZJpIWzZ. In this article, Carter describes his fellow elders as independent global leaders working together for peace and human rights.

18. Christine Dugas, "Gender pay gap persists," *USA Today*, October 24, 2012, http://www.usatoday.com/story/money/personalfinance/2012/10/24/gender-pay-gap/1652511/.

19. *CBS News*, 2/16/2013.

20. John 15:13.

21. Amos 5:24 (NIV).

SOMETIMES new ways of saying things provides a helpful perspective. Deb Hirsch is the team leader of Tribe of Los Angeles, an eclectic group of missional artists and vagabonds who meet as an intentional and unapologetic Jesus community. They meet on Sunday nights over dinner and wine. They value people. Their meetings follow this format: Talk about God, Read about God, Invite God to speak, Bless, and Eat. (Did you catch the acronym?) Deb lives life as a learner. She prefers leading from behind the scenes. She loves to train the people of God to really *be* the people of God. She travels globally, with her husband, Alan, breathing life into missional movements. Together, they helped found the Forge Mission Training Network and co-authored *Untamed: Reactivating a Missional Form of Discipleship.*[1] Deb empowers women and men: don't let valuable time be wasted; do what fits your gifting. If the structure or system you are in isn't something God has specifically called you to and graced you for, move on. This Aussie describes herself as a disrupter of the status quo...or was that a breath of fresh air?

CHAPTER 12
A CONVERSATION WITH ALAN HIRSCH

By Alan Hirsch and Felicity Dale

Respected across the church spectrum as a thought-leader and a key mission strategist, Alan Hirsch is in high demand as a speaker, and carries an extraordinary degree of influence through his many books. Alan is the founding director of Forge Mission Training Network and co-leads Future Travelers, an innovative learning program that helps megachurches become missional movements.

He told our team that whenever he's invited to speak, he takes the opportunity to expose the gender injustice that exists in the church and does whatever he can to promote women. We knew at that point that his voice needed to be heard in this conversation about women. I had the wonderful opportunity to interview Alan over the phone and was grateful for the insights he shared. Here is our conversation.

FELICITY: Alan, I know you take every opportunity you can to speak about the situation of women in the church. Why do you feel so strongly about this subject?

ALAN: When it comes to this issue of how women in the church have been treated over the course of history, we're probably dealing with one of the most long-standing, entrenched, and diabolical injustices of all time. It goes right back to the beginning of human experience, tracking to the Fall and the worst part of our broken humanity. It strikes a blow against the image of God in men and women.

Injustice toward women is still very deep-rooted in the life of the church. It infects who we are as God's people. Women are the backbone of so much that is good, and yet they have been marginalized over time—misrepresented and hated and scorned.

I often think of the Taliban in relation to this question. As Christians, we disapprove of the way the Taliban treats their women: "Their behavior is totally unacceptable. How can they treat other human beings like that? Their women have no legal status; they're barely visible people; they are not even allowed to show their faces; they have no rights."

We need to look at ourselves and see the traces of Talibanism in the church's treatment of women.

FELICITY: Have you always felt so strongly about injustices toward women? Was there anything specific that caused you to think this way?

ALAN: I've always had a great respect for women in general, but theologically, I've certainly changed somewhat. I was brought to the Lord in very conservative circles, and I assumed that their standard views on everything were correct, including their attitude toward women. When you come to the Lord, you tend to accept the scripting of the church, and, in Australia, gender was more of a non-issue.

Women contribute immensely to the life of the church, and I remember thinking it didn't make sense to hold them back in any way. On the contrary, why wouldn't I want to support both women and men to be everything God intends for them? It was a slow dawning of realization that women were not treated well by the church.

Because of the contrast with Australia, where the topic doesn't feature in the conversation, the sense of injustice was triggered for me by coming to America. Over here it's such a huge issue. I wasn't even aware of the phrase "complementarian or egalitarian" before I came to America five years ago. Maybe I just missed it. I think the Bible is nuanced toward a more subtle option, and not simply one or the other, and so I don't think they are particularly useful categories.

It's funny… most men, if you ask them, would acknowledge that they married up. I'm just one of the few men willing to make that more of a general statement.

FELICITY: Did your view of the Scriptures on this subject change over the years?

ALAN: I stand deeply within the conservative, evangelical understanding of Scripture. No one has ever been able to accuse me of being liberal. Acceptance of the fundamental authority of Scripture for all matters of life and faith is very much part of who I am.

We are Gospel people who define ourselves by the evangel. The Gospel itself is the hermeneutical key and guide to how we understand everything we do. Our appreciation of the Gospel, the "evangelion," is how we assess every issue, including women, slavery, racism, and all the things we face in society. Gender is just one of the issues.

I don't understand how a true evangelical can claim to appropriate the Gospel in all its fullness and countenance, and tolerate, for example, racism. So if someone questions me on issues like these, here's what I say:

"Can you imagine a situation in heaven, when Jesus is fully King, and God reigns completely, where people are traded as slaves—bought and sold as other people's property?"

People reply, "Of course not. There's no way that would happen in heaven."

And then I say, "Racism: can we conceive that in heaven there will be some kind of hierarchy of race in heaven?"

Everyone says, "Absolutely not!"

Then I take it to the issue of gender. I say, "Can you foresee a situation in heaven when you stand before God, that women are inferior in status or function to men?"

It would be very hard to hold a belief in the inferiority of women in light of the weight of glory. Of course I'm reflecting Galatians 3:28

here: "There's neither Jew nor Greek, slave nor free, male nor female, but Christ is all in all." (paraphrase).

The standard categories we use to analyze and separate ourselves from each other are done away with in Christ. In other words, in Jesus, all those distinctions that formerly defined us are abolished. As a Jew, I can no longer take the Jewish distinction as my primary identity or as allowing me to see myself as being in any way superior in the way I relate to other races. These categories, which formally defined and identified me, have been done away with in Christ. In Jesus, race is secondary at best.

The people of God are meant to live in a Kingdom reality. "May your Kingdom come on earth as it is in heaven." (Matt. 6:10, paraphrase). We're meant to embody what the Kingdom stands for and make it real now. If we're the ones who are to model what the ultimate heavenly reality is going to be, then we can't avoid the gender issue, because the Gospel does address it. That's the theological nub to me, the center. The evangel, the Gospel of Jesus Christ, does away with all the idols and false distinctions that people claim, and that must include one of the most fundamental definitions of all—male and female.

FELICITY: Do you think we're embodying the Kingdom or living out the Gospel when it comes to women—especially here in the USA?

ALAN: The church in the USA falls behind other Western countries in this. It's not doing a particularly good job of modeling an alternative way of life; it lags behind the general conscience of society.

In other countries, like Australia where I'm from, the status of women tends to be a non-issue. Even when people hold widely differing points of view, there's no belligerence or contention. Here in the USA, it's a hotly debated topic. When we arrived in the States, we were surprised to find it very much an issue, both within the culture and within the church itself. We can't avoid it and need to address it with grace, as brothers and sisters in civil discourse, because the missional implications are so huge.

Some men believe there's been a loss of identity for men—what it is to be a male—both in society and in the church. I agree. But I can't see that repressing the ministry of women makes them better men. Surely, the task of a godly person in Christ is to raise others up to their fullest possible potential in Jesus.

FELICITY: What do you think the church's attitude toward women says to society?

ALAN: I like the definition of the church being a sign, symbol, and foretaste of the Kingdom of God. It seems to me, in this area of gender, we're doing a woeful job. Why would any intelligent woman want to become a Christian if she's given the impression her potential in the church will be severely limited, or that because of her gender, it will be harder to achieve her God-given destiny?

Women currently have little choice but to serve in the peripheral ministries—being someone's personal assistant, running a women's ministry or ladies' Bible study. It's a limitation of human potential, and not good news for women. In fact, it's pretty bad news in my opinion. How would men feel if this was their lot? I simply cannot believe that this is all that Jesus intended for them. And sadly, it's shaped how non-Christians view the church in America.

FELICITY: Men like you carry a lot of influence. What can you contribute to changing the church's attitude toward women?

ALAN: It's time for men to step up significantly and be the voice on behalf of women. When women articulate these ideas, it often seems they're buttering their own bread, or that they're flaming feminists. It shouldn't be left up to women to advocate on their own behalf. It's time for the guys to stand up and be counted, to man up and defend the cause of those who don't have as much voice.

A lot of men would like to do this, but they fear the consequences or lack the means to do so. They're intimidated by the bully types with massive platforms that might tweet negatively about them and potentially ruin their ministry. A lot of men don't agree with the hardcore conservative approach, but because they can't articulate their arguments well enough, they stay silent. They feel alone and isolated against a well-organized opposition.

FELICITY: If a man will advocate on our behalf, it's seen differently. And men will often listen to another man they respect whereas they won't listen to a woman.

ALAN: We're all meant to stand up for others. First Peter 2:23, speaking of Jesus, says this: "He did not retaliate when he was insulted, nor threaten revenge when he suffered. He left his case in the hands of God, who always judges fairly." When we've been wronged, we shouldn't retaliate, but others in the body of Christ should take up the cause on our behalf; it's part of discipleship.

FELICITY: From a man's viewpoint, what do you see as the biggest barriers to women in leadership, and what can be done to overcome those barriers?

ALAN: One big challenge is the lack of visibility of female role models. Speaking on behalf of the missional conversation, women do some tremendous missional work on the ground and in my opinion are more natural, incarnational missionaries because of the importance they attach to relationships. Many women are great at engaging in society.

The problem comes in terms of symbolic representation. There are not nearly enough women who have a national platform, and I think something actively needs to be done about this. I don't want to sound paternalistic, but it's very much a man's world at the moment. Men need to create a platform for women with stories to tell, and those with the capacity to articulate should be given an opportunity to step onto that platform.

I often get criticism when the conferences I participate in feature all male speakers on the platform. But you don't want tokenism either. Including a woman just because of her gender would be paternalistic. At the same time, something needs to be done.

One of my friends runs a major conference, and people criticize him all the time for the lack of women speakers. He says to them, "If you can show me a woman who's making a visible impact and can communicate it on a large stage, I have no problem putting her on the platform."

The problem is, he can't seem to find many at all. A woman may have done something really significant in her local context, but few convert this into something of larger significance with real visibility and platform. I don't know one senior pastor of a large church who's a woman. How do you bring balance into that equation? It's a completely vicious cycle that will take a strategic response to correct. People need to come together to develop a plan to break that cycle.

Training options are very important. There should be forums where women are developed into senior leadership, or groomed and openly sponsored by men. Again, we need to be very wary of paternalism here, but something needs to be done.

FELICITY: I believe most women would welcome that. The group of women I work with formed because we recognized that nobody is mentoring women in positions of leadership. I'm not aware of many peer leadership groups at a regional or national level that include women. It's seen as inappropriate for a man to have a close relationship with women.

ALAN: So we are saved just to have male friends or female friends and that's it?! You can't have friends across the sexual boundary? We can never relate to 50 percent of the world's population? That isn't particularly good news! This can't be the restoration of all things that the Gospel points at. Surely, the salvation of Jesus and the Gospel brings us to a place where we can have healthy (and holy) relationships across the gender boundaries.

Of course men and women should be able to have relationships. They should watch the sexual dynamics—but we're meant to relate with the whole world. There need to be places where women are actually sponsored and mentored and coached by men. We need to very deliberately create forums for women.

There needs to be some theological backup too. The humanitarian arguments of liberal democracy don't convince Christians who know the language of the Scriptures. Genuine evangelicals haven't done enough good work in articulating the theology, and we need that. Scott McKnight, who is a major theologian, has just released a book on the subject of women called *Junia is Not Alone*. Did you know that Junia is a woman?

FELICITY: Yes, she's one of my heroines. One of my favorite books on this subject is *For Such a Time as This*[2] by British theologian, Martin Scott. It has a picture of a hand grenade on the front cover! In one of his footnotes, Martin disputes the fact that so many have said that Junia, who in Romans 12 is described as an apostle, is a man. He quotes theologian Peter Lampe as saying that Junia was a common feminine name at the time, with more than 250 references in the contemporary literature, but there is not a single one that refers to Junia as a man.[3]

We've sometimes talked about the women whose lives have been transformed by a genuine, heartfelt apology from men. If you were to voice an apology on behalf of men for the church's attitude toward women, what would you say?

ALAN: I get very emotional when I look at all the outright wickedness that has been perpetrated against women—the murders, the rapes, the marginalization, the indignities. I just want to cry at that point. It seems to me that it's necessary to make an apology and to repent on behalf of men. We men have misrepresented Jesus' heart and his purposes toward women and children. I think there's a real confession to make here. Honestly. I feel very sad and somewhat defiled and ashamed of being a man sometimes.

There's definitely sin to be confessed here. It goes way beyond the difficulties of Biblical interpretation to something that is deeply embedded and linked directly to the Fall and how sexuality is set up. Our gender awareness comes from a fallen understanding and needs a lot of redemption.

FELICITY: How do you feel the missional movement will be impacted if women are fully released and involved?

ALAN: The greatest secret weapon in God's hands is the people of God themselves. At least 50 percent of the population is comprised of females and so there's a huge missing piece in the equation when women are marginalized. I often point out that about 65 percent of leaders in China are women; in India, women are generating movements. The whole body of Christ needs to be activated to truly become the church we're called to be and extend God's purposes on the earth.

In the recent book, *On the Verge,*[4] that I wrote with Dave Ferguson, we refer to Daniel Pink's, *A Whole New Mind.*[5] He talks about the need to cultivate a more right-brained approach to leadership in ourselves and in our organizations. In right-brained thinking, beauty and esthetics bring a more artistic and emotional quality into the equation of design, narrative in story, seeing patterns, and discernment. Empathy, playfulness, and heart connection are very important too. These characteristics demonstrate a more feminine side of the brain. We need to somehow integrate a much more right-brained, feminine style and approach into organizational leadership.

Yes, we certainly need masculine technique and structure, but our movement needs to be more fluid and responsive and intuitive. If we're going to develop fully, we need the right-brained side too.

FELICITY: One of the things we're hoping this book will emphasize is that women bring entirely different characteristics to leadership.

ALAN: These are exactly the kind of qualities we need at this stage. When you're dealing with highly educated people, command and control clearly doesn't work. You have to convince people and engage them in the journey. So we need female approaches to leadership that will complement the male approaches.

FELICITY: Most women who are currently in church leadership tend to use a masculine style and approach to leadership because that's the way they get in.

ALAN: Dave Gibbons (founding pastor of New Song Church) says, when you look at the leadership structures of churches in the West, they are dominated by white males, and that until we get a more multi-cultural flavor, and both men and women in leadership, we're never going to be able to truly follow the Holy Spirit. Men tend toward technique and methodology and structure—and that's necessary, but it's not sufficient. We're going to need more. The world is made up of men and women, and the church needs to be that way too.

Let me quote from the book, *On the Verge*: "No matter how we choose to interpret the Pauline text, it's clear in the New Testament and from history, that women bear together with men the image of God, are integrally part of the body of Christ, are fully empowered agents of the King, and are commissioned in their conversion to Jesus' ministry and Kingdom. It's high time to balance out the male dominance in church ministry and leadership. If we do not, we can expect more of the same (somewhat one-brained) results we're currently achieving."

FELICITY: Here's a tongue-in-cheek question: Do you think women should be ordained?

ALAN: Ordination, certainly the way we've practiced it, doesn't appear in the New Testament, except for the characteristic of laying on of hands. The idea of ordination is a very institutional understanding. Institutions ordain. We created the dilemma in the first place because all the texts about female leadership in the church are attached to a notion that's not biblical. So if people ask me to make a case for the ordination of women, I'll say to them, "First you make for me a case for ordination from the Scriptures, and then I will make a case for women's ordination."

FELICITY: What about women in the five-fold gifts?

ALAN: Ephesians 4 gives us a wonderful opportunity to look at the issue of women in ministry with fresh eyes. When you look at the five-fold functions of apostle, prophet, evangelist, shepherd, and teacher in the book of Acts, you find all are fulfilled by both women and men, without any gender bias. It's a primary text in the constitution of the church that gives us a way beyond the current debate. Women play a role in every one of those gifts.

FELICITY: And if there are women apostles, prophets, and so on in the New Testament, it's hard to say they cannot lead.

ALAN: The logic in the Gospel is for the complete gender liberation of women. The Gospels point toward that, even if it couldn't be done fully back then. It's the same with slavery. Slavery wasn't done away with fully in the New Testament, but the seeds of its destruction were definitely sown. The Gospel, taken seriously, must logically conclude the end of slavery. We know that race is done away with. Logic must lead to women being liberated too. Were there female leaders in the New Testament? Yes! Look at Lydia, who ran a house church.

The book of Ephesians expresses Paul's best ecclesiology, the most concentrated understanding of the church. We tend to read it as a group of leaders studying in a seminary. Or we assume it was written to us in the twenty-first century. But it was written to the churches in Ephesus. They might have been a group of 20 or so house churches that had only been together for two years, and they get a letter from Paul. He's addressing all the other issues in the Kingdom—gender and race and slavery. Both men and women together are the intended recipients and hearers of the text. It's not a leadership summit or seminary; it's just a group of standard hacks, listening to a letter being read. If you take it that way, Ephesians 4:7, "to each one of us is given..." literally means that to each and every one present, a gift or vocation is given, and Christ is the one apportioning it. He gave these ministries for the building up of the body of Christ. It's not primarily a leadership text at all.

If we think of the church differently, not as an institution but as a movement, and if we see the church as made up of five-fold giftings, it becomes so full of energy. Every person is in the equation. Women are here and so are slaves. It's a radical text.

FELICITY: I'd like to go on the record and say to you that we're very appreciative of the fact that you always publicly stand up for women. Thank you, Alan.

Discussion Questions

1. Alan has a particular platform. Where in life do you have a "platform" or place of influence?

2. How can you use that place of influence to further the Kingdom of God or to stand against gender injustice?

3. How can you use your place of influence to help others reach their full potential in Christ? Is there anything specific you can do to help women?

4. What will you do this week to encourage both men and women to envision beyond the stereotypical gender roles endorsed by the American church?

Chapter 12 Notes

1. Alan and Debra Hirsch, *Untamed: Reactivating a Missional Form of Discipleship,* (Grand Rapids: Baker Books, 2010).

2. Martin Scott, *For Such a Time as This: The Liberation of Women to Lead in the Church,* (London: P.S. Promotions Ltd., 2001).

3. Ibid: 62.

4. Alan Hirsch and Dave Ferguson, *On the Verge,* (Grand Rapids: Zondervan, 2011).

5. Daniel H. Pink, *A Whole New Mind: Why Right-Brainers Will Rule the Future,* (New York: Riverhead Trade, 2006).

MICHELE PERRY simply took God at his Word, was willing to follow him anywhere, and ended up first in India, then South Sudan. This plucky, brave lady has spent the last six years of her life bringing God-potent love as a solution to injustice in South Sudan. Ordained and sent out by Heidi and Rolland Baker (of missionary organization Iris Global), she and Jesus opened a home to broken, orphaned, and desperate children, infusing them with worth and value. More than 100 little lives in war-torn southern South Sudan delighted to call her "Mama." The challenges, blessings, and miracles she experienced while living in the bush are profound. But, there's more—Michele was born without a left hip or left leg. She faced her own seemingly insurmountable obstacles, and God is bringing transformation to one of the most dangerous places on earth. These adventures in surrender and trust are captivatingly chronicled in her book, *Love Has a Face.*[1] What could total surrender look like in your life?

CHAPTER 13

THE INVISIBLE WOMAN SYNDROME

By Katie Driver

Injustice is often a thief of dignity. Many times when I was younger, people would approach my husband and me, and then engage Tony in conversation while totally ignoring me. It was as if I didn't exist. As the male half of the partnership, Tony was the significant one; I was unseen and unheard. This wasn't deliberate. When men (and women) want to communicate something, they reach out to the person they think is important—usually, the man. The woman is often left on the sidelines.

Do we have a right to be seen and heard? Perhaps in the Kingdom the answer is no—at least not for our own sake. Jesus made himself of no reputation and became a servant.[2] He didn't seek out recognition. But should we be fighting for the dignity of others? I believe the answer to that is yes.

I have a friend who is a recognized leader in her denomination. One day, she was the only female in a meeting with several men, when some strangers walked in. They gave her a cursory nod and then introduced themselves to the guys. It didn't take long for the newcomers to notice that the other men deferred to my friend. Finally, one of them asked, "Who ARE you?" She replied, "I'm just a mother in the church."

Sometimes within a church leadership context, men act as if women don't exist. It's not deliberate rudeness, but their conversation is often about things that men are interested in, leaving women with little to contribute.

Most women have experienced the indignity of being ignored because of our gender. Katie Driver has. She is a highly talented leader with apostolic and pro-phetic gifts whom God uses in remarkable ways, not just in this country but in other nations too. Here, she shares reflections on feeling like the invisible woman.

"**L**ook at me!" When my children were young, every day was filled with the endless activities that are common to young families. During those years, I continually felt like I didn't have enough hours in the day to do all I needed to. Throughout the day, I would answer my children's questions, play and read with them, feed and bathe them—all things that a mom can do without really paying attention. When I wasn't paying real attention to them, my kids would grab my cheeks between their little hands, pull my face up close to their own and say, "Mommy, look at me!"

There are many women who are planting churches, making disciples, teaching, preaching, training, and doing all kinds of ministry with both men and women, but who often remain invisible to us because they are outside the traditional roles women play. Until we consciously look for them, and recognize their presence in unfamiliar roles—they will remain invisible.

Mother's Day Scriptures

Most of us who have been Christians for any length of time are familiar with the words of Proverbs 31:10-31, which speak of a meritorious woman. These verses extol the virtues of a woman who takes excellent care of her household, who never sits idle but is busy with many activities—all of which bring honor to her husband and family. I have loved and appreciated these Scripture verses, commonly read on Mother's Day. They affirm and acknowledge the value of the roles of wife and mother (and some may also add business woman). I myself am a wife and mother who aspires to such praise.

However, we are probably less aware that these verses originated as an oracle taught by a woman (the mother of King Lemuel) to her son as he ruled. Her wisdom and advice was obviously worth something, since it is one of the most quoted chapters in the Bible regarding women. Yet we don't acknowledge her as the author—she remains invisible unless we look closely to see where these verses originate.

Women like to speak of Deborah, especially if the issue of leadership arises, but men are probably less aware of her role and success as a judge and leader of Israel during tumultuous, oppressive times.

Barak, the leader of the army, was willing to defer to her and wanted her commitment to join him in battle before he would proceed.[3] And how about Jael, who actually won this battle that had Barak so worried? She courageously and boldly pounded a stake through the head of the enemy's leader by playing the role of a hospitable and inconsequential woman. Have you heard much teaching about her significance, bravery, and action?

Unfortunately, there are many women in the Bible whom we don't hear about on Mother's Day, or any other day, because they don't fit in the traditionally female roles of wife and mother.

I remember an incident with a pastor who rejected my application as a church planter. When I questioned him about it, he replied that while I exhibited the needed gifts and skills for church planting, I was a woman and therefore not allowed to take that role. Since my husband did not have the necessary gifts, we were rejected.

"Well, what do you do with Deborah in the Bible?" I asked.

"Deborah was an exception," he replied.

"How do you know I'm not an exception?" I said.

That was the end of our conversation. Sadly, I realized if I wanted to use the gifts God gave me, it would have to be outside of this denomination.

Capacities

There are many biblical examples of non-traditional roles for women—this doesn't diminish the importance of traditional roles, but rather enlarges a woman's capacity to be used in many ways by the God who created her. However, seeing and recognizing these women is a challenge, because they often seem invisible unless we really look for them.

The Apostle Paul saw the capability of the women around him. He supported them in roles of significant influence and impact for the work of spreading the Gospel of Jesus. He seemed to value and appreciate the many ministries of women, and their capacity to function in multiple roles of influence and lasting fruit. Many times, he singled out the women who were his co-workers in ministry. They went far beyond the domestic role we generally ascribe to women of those times. Paul says of Euodia and Syntyche, "they have struggled beside me in the work of the Gospel, together with Clement and the rest of my co-workers, whose names are in the book of life."[4] Priscilla, Lydia, Mary, Phoebe, and Junia are a few of those co-workers.

It intrigues me that Paul is often accused of limiting the roles of women. I see him as a man who empowered and affirmed the women he came into relationship with. As good as it is to commend the woman that Proverbs 31 addresses, we also need to acknowledge that women function in far more roles than those of wife and mother, and with as much faithfulness, fruit, and honor. If we assume that a commendable woman is only to be found in the image of Proverbs 31, our assumptions will dictate what we see. We may be looking at a woman and not seeing her at all because she is not in her assumed role. We might be looking right at a Deborah.

Seeing is Believing

Five of us entered the home of a pastor in Spain and introduced ourselves as we sat at the dining table. He had invited our team from the United States, through the recommendation of a mutual friend, to come and minister for a week. As we ate lunch together (served by his wife), he began to discuss the ministry he wanted us to do in the upcoming week. He chatted away, giving us details of his desire to reach specific neighborhoods with the Gospel, the needs of his congregation for healing and deliverance, and his hopes that they would be stirred into greater faith and outreach into the community. He kept directing himself to each of the four men on my team, asking questions in hopes of eliciting a response that would clearly reveal to him which one of them was the leader.

As the pastor continued to direct his questions and attention to the men, they would turn and defer to me for a response. I would then step in and answer his questions. The pastor would nod and then go back to addressing the men. It became almost comical that he didn't seem to see or understand that none of the men at the table was the leader he was looking for. I was the leader of this team. However, I was a woman. I was not the one he assumed would be the leader; therefore, he continued to ignore all the obvious indications to that fact. He saw me, listened to me, but failed to really see me because he assumed the leader had to be a man.

This scenario played out all afternoon. It wasn't until I preached a message on the first night of ministry and many received salvation, others found healing and deliverance from demonic oppression, and there was the obvious affirmation of the Holy Spirit, that I started gaining credibility and the acknowledgment of my leadership from this pastor.

Many of us, as women, experience this on a regular basis when we minister in traditionally male leadership roles. We face not only the assumptions that limit us to certain roles and abilities, but also a high ceiling of credibility.

I serve as a regional contact for people who want to know more about the paradigm and practice of simple, organic, and missional church. Recently, I spent a few hours with a pastor of a traditional church in my city who wanted to incorporate some simple church practices into his church. I spent time pointing out pertinent Scriptures, the theology of the paradigm, answering his questions, and encouraging his own journey.

"Katie, this is great!" he said to me. "Do you know, is there someone in this area who could come and teach this stuff to my leaders?"

I sat stunned, collected myself, and said a prayer for grace before I responded. What I wanted to respond with was, *Wait! Did I hear you right? Hello? She has been sitting right across from you these last two hours!* Instead, I recognized the "Invisible Woman Syndrome" and told him about a few male trainers.

Assumptions

What we believe matters! All of us go throughout our day acting on assumptions we expect to be true. The power of our assumptions to influence our behavior is reinforced by experience. We even look for situations that support what we think. This drive to prove our assumptions true is so strong that even a contradictory experience may be reinterpreted to validate what we have assumed.

For example, a student used to getting A's on assignments may assume he always does A-grade work. If he receives a D instead, with notes from the professor addressing the poor quality of the work, this does not fit his assumption. The student reinterprets the grade and comments, and decides the professor was antagonistic about the subject matter, resulting in an undeserved low grade.

A similar effect is seen with women in leadership. We have many assumptions regarding leadership—they usually exclude the characteristics we attribute to women and esteem the ones we attribute to men. *The Onion,* a popular satire newspaper, posted a humorous example of the power of assumptions: "Man Finally Put In Charge of Struggling Feminist Movement."[5] It illustrates the assumption that male leaders are effective, powerful, and produce results, while female leaders are left lacking. What makes satire so good is that it contains elements of truth in its cultural criticism and uses irony to make a point. Here is an excerpt from the article:

'With a charismatic, self-assured guy like Pete pulling the strings, we might even see a female elected president one of these days,' said Nathan Roth, an analyst at the Cato Institute. 'Finally, the feminist movement has a face that commands respect.'

McGowan, however, said he didn't get into the business of women's rights for the praise.

'What these women were able to accomplish with the little manpower they had is very impressive,' McGowan said. 'I just bring a certain something to the table—I'm not sure what—that gave us that extra little push into complete female independence. I guess it just comes naturally.'

But despite his modesty, McGowan continues to garner praise from those closest to the cause.

'The whole movement just seems more legitimate with Buck in charge,' leading feminist Gloria Steinem said at a gala dinner Friday. 'His drive, focus, and determination are truly remarkable. Mr. McGowan is a man with a plan.'

We can laugh at this satirical article, but it sadly represents what most women in traditionally male roles face on a daily basis, and the bias against a feminine leadership style. Not only that, but it humorously illustrates how exceptionally difficult it can be for women to gain credibility.

When I introduce myself to a class of 24 students as their motorcycle-riding instructor, I often see a smirk on many of the men's faces. I can read their faces easily enough because I see it all the time. The "look" communicates something like this: *How could this feminine, attractive woman teach me anything about riding a motorcycle? You've got to be kidding me! You're my instructor?*

As the classroom part of the instruction progresses, it begins to dawn on some of these men that maybe I actually do know something about riding motorcycles. However, it isn't until after I have given a few riding demonstrations that I am granted the credibility that my husband (an instructor along with me) is given instantly because he is male. Whereas I have to gain their respect, he only has to lose it.

I know other female motorcycle instructors who "dummy down" their femininity and learn to walk, talk, dress, and teach like the men they work with. It gives them a head start in gaining credibility. If a woman happens to be attractive, credibility is even harder to achieve because of an assumption that attractiveness and leadership abilities can't go together.

What Society Sees versus What God Sees

Are the common male characteristics depicted in *The Onion* satire really what it takes to be an impacting and powerful leader? Is it so hard to imagine that femininity also has incredible power and strength in the realm of leadership, and that it doesn't require looking and acting like a man?

Much has been done in recent years to get men in touch with their "feminine side," to suppress little boys' aggressive social play, to add as much "fe" to the word "male" as possible. Some assert that men and women are the same, that any differences we may perceive are strictly cultural stereotypes. Our culture is working hard in many ways toward androgyny in male and female characteristics. But I believe God desires to use our male and female uniqueness to bring about the complete expression of humanity. It's not about becoming homogenized; it's about fully appreciating how God created us.

Women in leadership roles shouldn't have to look, think, speak, react, and align themselves with leadership traits and qualities that are predominantly masculine in order to be seen. The way our culture has defined leadership, and the way it is modeled both in the secular world and in the church, is almost completely male in its characteristics. However, is this the leadership style the Bible upholds? I don't believe so. Biblical leadership is less about who we are, and more about the One who truly sees us and calls us according to our unique makeup. God chooses people, male and female, who will respond to him in obedience, and he uses their individual traits and personalities to accomplish his divine purposes.

As we've already noted, the Bible provides several examples of women who embraced both their femininity and strength to serve God. There are also examples of men whom God used, not only because of their strength, but also in their vulnerability, and perhaps more so because of their willingness to be submissive. God sees value in what others often miss.

King David was a bold, often aggressive, certainly courageous male leader, but we see how vulnerable he became when he stripped down and danced semi-naked in worship before God and those watching. God called David when he was just the youngest son of a common shepherd and unimpressive to everyone else. God *saw* David and raised him up to be king, saying, "I have *found* David son of Jesse, a man after my own heart. He will do everything I want him to do." (Acts 13:22, emphasis added.) One cannot read the Psalms without seeing the soft, emotional, and vulnerable side of David. But it certainly did not diminish his leadership or his masculinity. In fact, God did not allow him to build the temple because he had "shed much blood and waged great wars."[6]

God also found something in Moses that others didn't, even Moses himself. He was trained and educated in the teachings of Egypt, and yet he described himself to God as someone who couldn't speak well. Instead, God saw a broken man he could use, one who didn't rely on his education and training, one who had an obedient heart that would do as he commanded.

The Apostle Paul was seen in a special way by God as well. He clearly was criticized in his leadership and said to have lacked the qualities associated with leadership in his day. He said to the

Corinthians, "For some say, 'His letters are weighty and forceful, but in person he is unimpressive and his speaking amounts to nothing.'"[7] Yet God chose him to bring the Gospel to the Gentiles.

Jesus himself defines a leader as being like an inconsequential slave—serving humbly, giving up one's own agenda for the sake of serving others. He warns against culturally accepted models and practices of leadership saying, "Woe to you when all men speak well of you, for their fathers used to treat the false prophets in the same way."[8]

Viewed in this light, maybe the Invisible Woman Syndrome is actually producing leaders who have decided not to promote themselves, nor seek out platforms and titles. This is far more in line with what the Scriptures teach us than our cultural model and practices we see in the world today. In some cases, choosing to stay behind the scenes may be how God asks us to make an impact.

Jesus was born in a stable, son of a young woman with no status, adopted son of a common carpenter. He astounded those around him, causing them to exclaim, "Isn't this Joseph's son?" They only saw Jesus at face value and couldn't compute how he spoke with such authority. Jesus did not look like the leader people were expecting.

Similarly, some people may find it difficult to believe that God would choose a woman to walk in leadership gifts usually accredited to men. But if we would look and really see these "invisible" women all around us, we will recognize that God does choose women—he sees their value. A woman never has to say to God: "Look at me!" He always sees. Isn't it time for us to do the same?

Discussion Questions

1. Women: Have you ever felt invisible? What was the setting? What feelings did you experience? What did you think? How did you respond?

2. Men (or women): Have you ever ignored or minimized women as less important than men? What should you do about this?

3. How does God minister to you in those circumstances? What biblical characters encourage you?

4. What changes can be made so your daughters can be seen and your sons can be free from gender bias?

Chapter 13 Notes

1. Michele Perry, *Love Has a Face,* (Ada: Chosen Books, 2009).

2. Philippians 2:5-8.

3. Judges 4–5.

4. Philippians 4:2-3 (NRSV).

5. "Man Finally Put In Charge Of Struggling Feminist Movement," *The Onion,* December 2007, http://www.theonion.com/articles/man-finally-put-in-charge-of-struggling-feminist-m,2338/.

6. 1 Chronicles 22:8.

7. 2 Corinthians 10:10 (NIV).

8. Luke 6:26 (NASB).

PART FIVE

CREATING A CULTURE OF CHANGE

MINA MILLEN was raised in a Muslim home. She found a relationship with Christ after her parents moved the family from Cyprus and enrolled her in a Christian elementary school. When Mina and her husband became discontented with "church as usual," they sought deeper fellowship with other believers. Mina's search led her to a ministry called Luke 10. Its leader, John White, shared with Mina a concept called CO2—Church of Two. It represents Christian fellowship at its most basic level: two or three believers thriving together in relationship with Jesus. Church happens daily, not just once a week. Mina first shared the CO2 concept with her Bible study leader, and then offered the concepts at a ladies' retreat. It spread from there. Some practice CO2 in the car or on the phone. Others are teaching their kids to hear from God. Moms and daughters are meeting together. So are teenagers. Larger listening groups have formed. Dozens of couples in a marriage group are now incorporating this simple way to go deeper with each other and hear from God. Mina has personally shared Luke 10 principles with more than 200 others so far, and feels that her call is to "salt" the CO2 concept wherever the doors open. She wants to help others gain confidence in hearing from God and responding in joyful obedience. And it all started with a simple thirst.

CHAPTER 14

THE EMANCIPATED WOMAN

By Suzette Lambert

Years of being taught (at least by implication) that women are second-class citizens of the Kingdom—that God has imposed limits and boundaries on women— have had an effect. Some women have become passive spectators, fearing that if they initiate rather than wait for a man to lead, they are stepping outside God's will. Others find it a source of great pain, wondering, "Why would God create me with these gifts only to frustrate me by not being able to use them in the church?" Others (both men and women) have voted with their feet over this issue and left the church. Men are victims too. The vast majority are not being deliberate misogynists—they have been taught these same things. The result is a crippled church.

Our team often receives email from other women that talk about the ongoing hurts they face simply because of their gender. Like the female missionary whose mission board expects her to simply support her husband (who's out doing the "real work" for the Kingdom). Or the church worker who sent this message: "As a woman, I often feel that simply because of my gender I have an unforgivable/unwashable sin hanging onto me..." Or the ones who feel called by God to use their gifts but are excluded from various roles because they are female. Men are often unaware that women have been deeply hurt by the church system. It's not that they don't care; it's just not on their radar. It's vital that women find healing. Until they do, they may limit how God can use them.

When a woman realizes that God is not oppressing her, but has come to set her free, will she let God heal her, or will she choose to become bitter? Our team member, Suzette Lambert, understands this well, for she was once there herself. She had to heal from the grievous mistake of feeling like a second-class citizen. As a result of this process, she is now helping others. Suzette is a licensed marriage and family therapist and helps people heal from life's injustices.

My husband sent me a striking painting he bought in Afghanistan. The first thing that caught my eye was the vibrant, blue cloth draped over a stool, on which sat a birdcage. Then, with a shock, I realized it wasn't a stool—it was the head of a woman, given only the holes in a piece of blue cloth through which to see the world outside her burka. She was as trapped as the bird in the cage on her head.

While we women in the West may not wear burkas, we do wear the restrictions imposed on us by our own culture. Our minds trap us just as effectively as a burka. We are restricted by our own accepted norms. Not only that, but some of us have been hurt and damaged by a patriarchal church system that limits us from being everything God has called us to be.

Some of us have been victims of leaders who crave power/control.

Some of us have lost hope that anything will change.

Some of us have left the church as a result.

Gender Realities

All of us are constantly aware of our gender. As women, we have no ability to think of ourselves as anything other than women. The same is true for men. When faced with the opposite gender, we know we are different. Men are usually physically stronger than women; women are more intuitive. When we are with others of the same gender, we notice our sameness as well as our differences.

Prejudice is part of the price of being female. Our very gender has been a betrayal point for us. The subjugation of women is an attack on our very being. As we move away from our burkas, where do we go?

Some women respond to being marginalized by demanding recognition. A woman may decide that becoming like a man in her delivery will give her the power she desires. She may be angry, presenting herself as pushy and desiring control. She always appears to have ulterior motives, a need to be acknowledged and powerful.

Power and control are the wrong motives for leadership of either gender.

What we need is not revenge, but healing. If we don't go through the healing process, we run the danger of becoming like our abusers, committed to control and power. If we don't receive healing, we may remain trapped under our burkas, never moving into the fullness of destiny God has for us. But if we allow Jesus to heal our wounds, we can fulfill our calling as women of God—set free from the restrictions, the birdcage of the past, to do and be everything he calls us to.

The Results of the Fall

In graduate school, I learned that we only heal within relationship. The greatest and most healing relationship we have in our lives is with God. Adam and Eve ate the fruit in the garden. The result? Their relationship with God was broken and they hid from him. To add to it, Adam left his initial role of dominion over the garden and turned his attention to controlling Eve.

Eve carried great shame as a result of the Fall. Shame causes a breakdown of relationships; it makes us want to hide those parts of us that are hurt, afraid that somehow we will be damaged further if we expose them. Part of healing is stripping away the shame and deciding to move past it to a place of vulnerability.

We may be women who have been hurt by the way the church, or people within the church, have treated us because of our gender. How can we break out of the cage we are trapped in? How can we remove our burkas?

When we realize the truth of our situation—that we are victims of injustice and gender bias—what we do in response makes a huge difference to the final outcome in our lives.

Allowing God to Heal

Vulnerability involves a dialogue between God and us. It can go something like this:

> Search me O God and know my heart, try me and know my anxieties, and see if there is any wicked way in me, and lead me into the way everlasting.[1]

This prayer allows God to address the pain—the places of fear and hurt left as the result of an abusive system. It's very simple, but it takes people into a greater understanding of his love. Why? It gives God permission to heal our wounds and to correct our faulty thinking.

Usually, the first thing God does is to reveal his character, rewriting who we believe him to be. Maybe we saw him as part of the problem, thinking it was God who failed us; it was his fault our gender prevented us from having the same rights as others, from being a full heir to the Kingdom. God will address and correct our faulty perceptions, assuring us of his unconditional love.

I remember a time in my life when all God did was address my fears in the long hours I spent with him. It was wonderful and terrible at the same time. I came out of it liking me more and loving him without question. It was a great wilderness time and very necessary for where I am now. I would not trade those times for anything.

The second thing God does is to address our pain. Being his child means he wants to tend to our wounds. When a child is hurt, a parent looks at the wound and says, "Let's put on a Band-Aid." Maybe first aid isn't adequate to deal with the problem and the child needs a doctor or hospital. What a privilege that we get to do this with our caring, heavenly Father, who always has our best interests at heart. His love for us is unfathomable.

One day, I was on my way to lunch with a wonderful woman several years older than I was. She had been in the church for many years and loved Jesus. The Lord spoke to me very specifically, saying, "Tell her that I love her."

I argued with him: "Surely she must know that. She's more mature than I am and she's been your child for years." Yet the Lord was very adamant about what I was to say. Through the years, I've learned not to fight God, so I resolved to tell her.

When I arrived at the restaurant, I told her that God loved her. She disagreed with me, somehow convinced that God loved everyone in the world, but not her personally, as an individual. To her, he had always been the God that was "out there, at a distance." But when she understood what God was saying to her, when she accepted his love, her life changed.

Beauty for Ashes

For most of us, healing represents relief from our pain. So the healing process becomes more of a meandering than an actual path that can be easily adhered to. It's helpful to have decided in advance what healing looks like.

I am committed to Isaiah 61:3:

To console those who mourn in Zion, To give them beauty for ashes, The oil of joy for mourning, The garment of praise for the spirit of heaviness; That they may be called trees of righteousness, The planting of the Lord, that He may be glorified. (NKJV)

What qualities do we want to possess as we pursue the healing process? I know God delights to give beauty for ashes—it's one of his specialties. So what "beauty" do we want to come through the process of healing to replace the "ashes" that have contaminated our lives? Do we want to be more gracious? Do we want more love? Do we want more wisdom? What qualities do we want to replace the hurt and injustice we have carried from the systems that pushed us into being a lesser expression of our true selves? God delights when we ask him.

What is the "beauty" that we want? What "ashes" are we willing to let go of?

The Most Important Key

I have a friend who says that walking in unforgiveness is like drinking poison and expecting the other person to die. Forgiveness does not mean we forget; it just means we release, we let go, and choose not to act in a vengeful way toward those who have hurt us. How do we forgive those who have used control to gain power over us? How do we release the feeling of being unable to live up to the religious mark? Are we willing to release the bitterness and hurt that may have become a part of our lives? Are we using our past hurts as something to hold onto, legitimizing our right to be bitter and angry with our words? Letting go can be the hardest part of the healing process, and it may take some time.

To live in the past is foolish and to live in the future is impossible. When we live with unforgiveness, we are stuck in either the past or the future. Unforgiveness makes us constantly aware of our past wounds and we adjust our lives accordingly. Unforgiveness causes us to project into the future how some act on our part may right the situation, or how we may be vindicated when something bad happens to the person who hurt us. Forgiveness frees us from that thinking and releases us into our healing.

As we go through the healing process, we forgive the people who have hurt us. Who are the men, or perhaps even other women, who have worked to "keep us in our place" and used us to further their own agenda of subjugation and control?

What do we do when we have painful memories? We go to our Father with them. We get quiet. We talk to him, asking him to reveal the truth of who we are. There are key verses that can help with this. I love these positional statements that say who we are in Christ:

> How great is the love the Father has lavished on us, that we should be called children of God! And that is what we are![2]

> . . .to the praise of the glory of His grace, by which He made us accepted in the Beloved.[3]

Forgiving Ourselves

It's often easier for us to forgive others than it is to forgive ourselves. Perhaps we ask the question, "How could I have been so gullible?" or "What was I thinking?" We seldom give ourselves the grace we may afford another person.

God wants us to find peace with our past as well as finding his purpose in it. He uses the pain we have experienced. Perhaps it is a catalyst to help us press on into our gifts and calling. Perhaps we can use our experience to help others find their own healing. Perhaps we learned the great strength of perseverance, or patience, or a whole new level of forgiveness.

Healing through the Body of Christ

As we heal within, through our relationship with God, there is another place where we can find healing—through the corporate expression of a healthy group of believers. A group that is open and willing to see the body of Christ as a complete and perfect being, without segregating or viewing the female gender as somehow deformed or unimportant.

A fellowship that does not discriminate by gender, but celebrates differences while releasing each person into their God-given calling, can be an essential part of the healing process. Everyone is allowed the expression of the Holy Spirit, both within and outside of the group. Neither gender is threatened, nor is there any need to subjugate anyone within the group. We can share times of openness and vulnerability, our fears and hopes. As each person expresses the gifts the Holy Spirit has given them, the whole group has a greater experience of the presence of Christ.

It is from this place of wholeness that we can begin to raise our daughters and sons in a healthy way. Not only will children see women released in church, they will view this as normal in every area of life. Marriages will be healthier—complementary relationships, as opposed to relationships that are competing to win the subjugation battle. Imagine if a whole generation grew up never knowing gender bias in church or in life.

When a woman does well, she automatically acts as a role model that gives other women hope for their own success. If a woman is caught in the world of gender restrictions but wants freedom, can she find a mentor who is ahead of her in the process to walk through it with her? Someone who can come alongside and gently challenge her to think differently, who will encourage her in the gifts she has been given by her heavenly Father?

Facing our Fear in Seeking Justice

In Numbers 27, there is an account of five courageous women, the daughters of Zelophehad, who speak up for their inheritance. They were not afraid to express their predicament: their father had died leaving no sons. His name was about to disappear from among the clans unless they, his daughters, could inherit the land he was due. They fearlessly stood before Moses, Eleazar the priest, the tribal leaders, and the entire community to present their argument. What was the Lord's response?

> The claim of the daughters of Zelophehad is legitimate. You must give them a grant of land along with their father's relatives. Assign them the property that would have been given to their father.[4]

Not only did the Lord judge on behalf of these brave daughters, he made it a legal requirement for the future. God desires justice for women.

If we speak up when we face gender discrimination, we join the battle against injustice. If we go with a right attitude rather than a combative one, and if we seek to release others (not just ourselves), we will find that blessing follows, because our Father is always working for justice.

A woman named Abigail[5] defied the culture of her time and saved her household. Even though she disobeyed her husband's wishes, she did what was right in God's eyes when she gave David and his army the provisions her husband had refused to donate. In doing the right thing, she saved the men of her community—including her husband. Abigail took a stand for what she thought was right, but let the Lord deal with her husband.

How often do we fail to do the right thing because we are afraid and others suffer in consequence?

Doing the "right thing" varies in its outworking. Maybe it's teaching our children not to accept a world that counts one gender as less than another. Maybe it's concluding that the mother (or father) who stays at home has as important a job as those who work outside of the home. Maybe it's acknowledging that the differences each gender displays are equally important—after all, God created them male and female.

Gender is merely a description of characteristics that are physical, as well as personality-oriented.

Life in the Spirit

One day, some Sadducees (who didn't believe in resurrection of the dead) came to Jesus and asked him a question about a man who died without having children. In turn, each of his six brothers followed the Law of Moses and married the man's widow, and each of them also died childless. The question the Sadducees asked Jesus was this: "In the resurrection, whose wife of the seven will she be?" Jesus replied, "In the resurrection they neither marry nor are given in marriage, but are like angels of God in heaven."[6] In the realm of the spirit, there may not be gender as we know gender. Jesus said, "True worshipers will worship the Father in spirit and truth."[7]

In the Kingdom of God, there is no room for minimizing a particular gender. When we teach the next generation of children, let's place our emphasis on the fact that we are spiritual beings having a human experience, rather than human beings having a spiritual experience. When we see ourselves as spiritual beings, we are able to see ourselves rising above our present circumstances, moving past gender prejudice into Kingdom living.

From Healing to Mentoring

Some of my greatest growth experiences have been in mentoring, and the more I grow in these areas, the more people the Lord sends my way. If I am willing to lay down my life, my plans, and my agenda to help others become the best they can be, they will soar and so will I. The mentoring process is neither rigid nor religious, but it's an enjoyable relationship where people know you love them and are honest with them. Jesus was very patient with his disciples, and they learned the most just from being with him. We so often want to structure things, that we forget the power of a relationship.

One of the best examples of one woman mentoring another comes in the Old Testament, in the book of Ruth. Naomi and her husband escaped a famine in Israel by moving temporarily to the land of Moab. When her husband died, Naomi was left with two sons, both of whom had married Moabite women. The two sons died as well, and Naomi gave her daughters-in-law the option of returning to their own people. One of them chose to do so, but the other, Ruth, clung to Naomi and refused to leave her. Ruth saw something in Naomi that she wanted to emulate, and Naomi was willing to mentor her, even to the point of taking her back to Bethlehem and introducing her to another husband. Naomi opened doors for Ruth that brought her into the ancestral line of the Messiah. What a success for both of them.

Opening the Doors

When women (or men) open doors for other women, it introduces possibilities for both of them. In the world, there is much competition, especially in the corporate world. Jesus addressed the competition factor and introduced the idea of servanthood as leadership.[8]

When someone serves in a way that opens the door for another woman, both are blessed. I have been involved in a particular ministry through the years. As a result, I have introduced many other women to this ministry too. It has given them an opportunity to become involved in Kingdom work, as well as to experience the fun of relationships with others. Their lives have become richer as a result, and so has mine.

St. Irenaeus said it best: "The glory of God is man fully alive." This includes women. When both genders express themselves in a "fully alive," fully unfettered way, everyone wins. When one gender is excluded, banished into a corner, everyone loses—both men and women.

Hidden in Christ

Will doing all of this remove our burkas? We may still remain hidden, but it won't be because of our clothing, our culture, or as a result of those who have badgered us into a cage. What we will find is this: we are hidden with Christ in God,[9] and from there, given more freedom than we ever thought possible. The church needs women as role models; we can fulfill (and help others fulfill) that function. As we stand against the status quo of the past, we can assist others in finding their own freedom. We will love and live more fully, enjoying others and ourselves along the way. We will have learned to serve by fighting injustice and leading other women into a wide-open place, where they can, in turn, help other women and men find their fullness in Christ.

Discussion Questions

1. Women: Are there people you need to forgive—those who made life difficult for you or mistreated you as a woman in ministry?

2. Men: Are there ways you've treated women because of what you were taught that you now regret? What can you do about this?

3. Are there other areas of freedom or restoration you would like to experience, particularly as they relate to gender roles in the church? What do you see as the next step forward?

4. Discuss the process of beauty replacing ashes (bitter or better) in your life or someone else's life you have observed.

Chapter 14 Notes

1. Psalm 139:23-24 (NKJV).

2. I John 3:1 (NIV).

3. Ephesians 1:6 (NKJV).

4. Numbers 27:7 (NIV).

5. 1 Samuel 25.

6. Matthew 22:23-32 (NKJV).

7. John 4:23.

8. Matthew 20:25-28.

9. Colossians 3:3.

AT AGE 57, Helen Esdaile thought her years of ministry were behind her. Struggling through many difficult, even wandering, years of practicing her faith, God amazingly "renewed her youth" through a prophecy, and began "restoring the years the locusts had eaten." God refreshed her with a future and a hope, and a powerful ministry to the broken and downtrodden began to unfold. Helen and her husband moved from a beautiful, rural Australian property where she hosted a bed and breakfast, to a nearby location derogatorily known as the "armpit of the South Coast" of New South Wales. The call was to minister compassion, mercy, service, and the Gospel to some of the most broken and hurting low socio-economic citizens of Australia. They purchased an old, run-down house and provided free meals or discounted groceries to those who lived on the streets or in deep poverty. They opened a second community center on the other side of town to serve a similarly depressed area. Even more importantly, their outreach, aptly called Australian Mercy, serves as an oasis of unconditional love and acceptance that offers new life and change.

CHAPTER 15
MEN OPENING THE DOOR— SUBMITTING TO WOMEN

By Michael Frost

Most men, in our experience, are not deliberately trying to exclude women, but they are often blissfully unaware that their attitude causes problems. They assume that because women are not kicking up a fuss, they must be content with the status quo. While that is sometimes true, for many women, there is an underlying frustration that they cannot use their leadership gifts in the place that matters so much to them—the body of Christ. As women, we're not trying to go it alone. We value the input of men in our lives. We appreciate when they open the door (of ministry) for us.

Let me give some examples. Every night for years, Katie Driver's husband, Tom, laid hands on her and prayed that God would bless and release her into ministry so she would reach her full potential and destiny. It's hardly surprising that Katie has a powerful ministry both in her region and in other nations. Tom is the quieter one of the two, and totally content for her to be in the spotlight more than he is.

Sometimes it's about sharing the spotlight. My husband, Tony, has opened doors for me by inviting me to the platform and encouraging me every step of the way.

Michael Frost is another "Barak" who is willing to stand up for women. He is an internationally recognized missiologist and one of the leading voices in the missional church movement. His books[1] are required reading in colleges and seminaries around the world, and he is much sought after as an international conference speaker. He is the founding director of the Tinsley Institute, a mission study center located at Morling College in Sydney, Australia. He was also one of the founders of the Forge Mission Training Network and founder of the missional Christian community Small Boat Big Sea, based in northern Sydney.

Like the other contributors to this volume, I don't believe God has given Christians a mandate to preserve and perpetuate cultural notions of masculinity and femininity. It is interesting to note that the church seems quite willing to abandon various other Ancient Near Eastern or Greco-Roman blind spots, like attitudes toward disability, race, and social class. And yet, certain sections of the contemporary church are deeply resistant to abandoning ancient attitudes to gender. Either we believe that, through Christ, God has given Christianity a redemptive, inclusive, good-news-for-the-least-of-these kind of feel, or we don't. And I do.

But it is pretty hollow when we guys say we stand for the inclusion of women in leadership roles, but then belong to teams comprised of all men, attend conferences at which only men speak, sit on all-male committees, and exclusively read books written by men. One of the important ways male leaders will encourage change in our churches is to model such change in our own lives and ministries. That means more than verbal or written affirmations. It means submitting to the leadership and insights of women and exhibiting such submission in the ways we speak about our lives and ministries. If people hear male leaders say we are encouraging women as leaders, they will understandably look for evidence of that in our lives. Are we learning from women? Are we being led by women? Are we modelling a more inclusive stance on gender in the church? Here are some ways that men who wish to affirm the role of women as teachers and leaders might do that.

Invite a Woman to be Your Mentor

If we are serious about affirming the role of women in our churches, then one small (but important) step could be to invite a woman leader to be your mentor, coach, or spiritual guide. (I use the word "mentor" as a cover-all term here.) When influential male leaders refer to their mentor with the feminine pronoun, it has extraordinary weight. In fact, it's a way of affirming inclusion without making a declarative statement. "Oh," we might say casually, "I was talking to my mentor about this issue the other day and she said…" Compare this to the more combative language from male leaders, who wish to affirm women's roles, but are never themselves led or taught by women. By inviting a mature, godly, woman leader to be your mentor, you normalize the idea of female leadership and focus on what she teaches you, not whether she should be allowed to teach in the first place.

Church leaders have expressed concern about mixed-gender mentoring, fearing that an intimacy might develop between the mentor and the mentee that leads to unhealthy attachment or sexual impropriety. This goes back a long way. Consider the deeply anxious approach of, say, St. Augustine toward women in his life. His friend, Possidius, described his conduct this way:

> No woman ever set foot in his house, he never spoke to a woman except in the presence of a third person or outside the parlour, he made no exceptions, not even for his elder sister and his nieces, all three of them nuns.[2]

Given what we know of Augustine's sexual predilections, he might have been simply erring on the side of caution, but this does not set a good example. His behavior indicates the presence of women to be an uncontrollable temptation to him, revealing his near-deification of women as objects of irresistible desire.

A hint of Augustine's approach can be seen in the later writings of Thomas Aquinas, who not only saw women as inferior beings, but believed women to be less resistant to sexual temptation than men, "because there is a higher water content in women, they are more easily seduced by sexual pleasure."[3] These attitudes are considered sexist today. And yet, much of the current anxiety expressed about cross-gender mentoring seems to draw on unspoken fears of the irresistibility of sexual desire. I prefer to assume that the modelling of good, healthy mentoring relationships across the genders is more important than buying into anxiety about the presence of women in your life.

I believe there is great wisdom to be gained from sitting at the feet of godly, mature men and women; we should not forbid receiving from one another simply because of gender. Billy Graham and Bill Bright were both mentored by Henrietta Mears; Loren Cunningham was profoundly impacted by the teaching of Joy Dawson; the Anglican charismatic renewal in England was guided in the early days by Jean Darnell, and the list goes on.

Having said that, there are nonetheless reasonable concerns about propriety in mixed-gender mentoring relationships. For these reasons, we should consider the following: not meeting alone or behind closed doors; gaining the approval of your spouse and your pastor or spiritual leaders; delimiting the areas of discussion to avoid sexual issues; addressing any attraction to the person quickly and decisively; staying accountable. But with some simple, common sense limits in place, there is no reason the church can't model what healthy cross-gender mentoring can look like.

Quote Regularly from Female Authors

When was the last time you heard a preacher quote from a woman theologian or writer? How often do you read scholarly articles that draw on the work of female theologians? If male leaders are going to model their affirmation of female leadership, they need to not only submit to their teaching but also liberally quote those female teachers whose work has shaped them. Unless we are reading and seriously engaging with women as writers and theologians, how can we say we affirm their role as teachers?

The following list is by no means exhaustive. It includes writers and theologians from a variety of theological positions. Read them. Even if you don't agree with them, when we quote them (even to differ with them) we model our preparedness to take women teachers seriously.

- Ellen T. Charry is professor of historical and systematic theology at Princeton Seminary, and the author of *By the Renewing of Your Minds: The Pastoral Function of Christian Doctrine*.[4]

- Sarah Coakley is a Church of England priest and professor of divinity at the University of Cambridge, UK, and the author of *Faith, Rationality and the Passions*.[5]

- Rachel Held Evans is a journalist, blogger, and the author of *Evolving in Monkey Town* and *A Year of Biblical Womanhood*.[6]

- Jen Hatmaker is a church planter and the author of multiple books, most notably *7: An Experimental Mutiny Against Excess*.[7]

- Carolyn Custis James is a writer, speaker, and activist. Her latest book is *Half the Church: Recapturing God's Global Vision for Women*.[8]

- Debra Hirsch is the pastor of Tribe of LA, a noted conference speaker, and the co-author of *Untamed: Reactivating a Missional Form of Discipleship*.[9]

- Ann Morisy is a British theologian and lecturer and the author of *Bothered and Bewildered*.[10]

- Nancey Murphy is a philosopher and theologian and the professor of Christian philosophy at Fuller Theological Seminary, Pasadena. She is the author of *Bodies and Souls, or Spirited Bodies?*[11]

- Jo Saxton is a director of 3DM, a church consultancy group, and the author of *Real God, Real Life: Finding a Spirituality That Works*.[12]

- Kathryn Tanner is professor of systematic theology at Yale Divinity School and the author of *Christ the Key*, and *Jesus, Humanity and the Trinity*.[13]

This is simply my off-the-top-of-my-head list. You will know of others. Read them. Take them seriously. Learn from them. Quote them.

Abandon Inaccurate Rhetoric about the Feminization of Church

"The stallions hang out in bars; the geldings hang out in church," says David Murrow in his influential book, *Why Men Hate Going to Church.*[14] Written in 2004, Murrow's book touched off a storm of articles and blog posts complaining about the so-called feminization of church. Murrow's argument, put simply, was that women are relational, nurturing, and peace-loving, whereas men are goal-driven, competitive, and adventurous. He says women thrive when secure, and men thrive when challenged. No proof of this is offered other than the author's observation, but on that basis, Murrow concludes that men hate going to church because it presents "feminine values and preferences," like love and emotions, and touchy-feely stuff, like repairing relationships.

No one has been more outspoken about this than Mark Driscoll, pastor of Seattle's Mars Hill Church. In his opinion, the church has produced "a bunch of nice, soft, tender, chickified church boys." He goes on to assess that "sixty percent of Christians are chicks, and the forty percent that are dudes are still sort of chicks."[15]

Driscoll and Murrow (and those who agree with them) have harped about the feminization of church so often and for so long now, that it is taken as a given these days by many younger church leaders. But where is the evidence? Driscoll would argue the fact that women make up 60 percent of the church in America proves his point. But the percentage of male leaders in church far and away outstrips that of women leaders. No doubt, in his estimation, most of those leaders are "chickified church boys." In his presentation at the 2006 Resurgence Conference, Driscoll announced that "real men" avoid the church because it projects a "Richard Simmons, hippie, queer Christ, that is no one to live for [and] is no one to die for." He then explained, "Jesus was not a long-haired…effeminate-looking dude," but had "calloused hands and big biceps."

Others seem to share Driscoll and Murrow's perspective. In an article entitled, "Why Men Stay Away from the Feminized Church," posted on the blog Wintery Knight, one person wrote,

> Many women also don't want to be confronted about their beliefs by informed men, because their beliefs are based more on intuition and emotion. They would rather be accepted and affirmed—and so they favor men who don't know much about the details of Christianity. So manly Christian skills: theology, apologetics, ethics, philosophy, history, science, etc., are not valued in the feminized church.[16]

Add to this inaccurate rhetoric, such outdated ideas as Thomas Aquinas' conclusion that women are less intelligent than men. As we saw earlier, the basis for his argument was that women have a "higher water content than men." He writes:

> Men have more perfect reason and stronger virtue than women. The intellectual defects of women are similar to those evident in children and mentally ill persons.[17]

This dialectic between soft/hard, emotional/logical, relational/practical, male/female, gets more mileage in church circles than it deserves, in my opinion. We can all think of men who confirm Driscoll and Murrow's stereotypes. But we can just as easily think of men who shatter the distinction. Also, many women are highly competitive, primarily left-brained and logical, and more focused on outcomes than feelings. By presenting culturally determined stereotypes as biblical teaching, we find ourselves on very thin ice. I think it's fair enough to suggest that a church that teaches and embodies love, relationships, emotions, kindness, and charity is not a feminized community. It makes no sense to suggest that prayer is a feminine activity, but apologetics and evangelism are male ones.

The Bible doesn't even hint that this is so, and therefore neither should we.

Furthermore, among American evangelical churches, 57 percent of members are women (regularly rounded up by Driscoll to 60 percent). That's within a reasonable range of a 50-50 split—not enough to cause the alarm many are sounding. Also, bear in mind that 93 percent of senior pastors in America are men, according to evangelical pollster George Barna. This hardly seems like a female takeover.

Nonetheless, in her book, *Total Truth: Liberating Christianity from its Cultural Captivity*, visiting Biola scholar, Nancy Pearcey, still suggests there is cause for concern. She says industrialization forced men to seek work away from home, in factories and offices, which created a split between the public and private spheres of life. The public sphere became secularized through the new values of competition and self-interest, and the private sphere came to represent the old values of nurturing and religion. Pearcey concludes religion came to be seen as for women and children, and not as relevant to the "real" world of business, politics, and academia.

It could be suggested that Pearcey presents a pretty simplistic reading of the situation. Even if it could be sustained, surely the effects she identifies with industrialization have been greatly ameliorated by the emergence of new technologies, flexible work hours—and especially the upheaval of the feminist movement and the flooding of the workplace by women. These are effects that have been reshaping America for half a century now.

What the church needs is more congregations with a vast variety of people, including those who confirm culturally prescribed gender stereotypes and those who shatter them. By arguing for one type or another we alienate the less preferable, which leads us to bear a false witness about the power of the Gospel to unite all people as brothers and sisters in Christ.

Handle Gender Differences Very Lightly

Sometimes it's fun to caricature people with stereotypes. After all, they're called stereotypes because a lot of people fit them. I'm a middle-aged Aussie male, a Gemini, an INTP on the Myers-Briggs profile, and my Enneagram number is five. Give me a second and I'll find my top five strengths in the StrengthsFinder questionnaire. Do your best at figuring me out. It's fun to play with that stuff. But, surely we as Christians must affirm our belief that all human beings are fearfully and wonderfully made, we are rich, complex, deep, and in many respects, unfathomable creatures. The attempt to box people in with simplistic descriptions is a form of objectification that we should all resist. Introvert. Right-brained. Calvinist. Republican. Et cetera. There's more to everyone than the label, even if the label says something about us.

Likewise with gender stereotypes. I suggest we handle them very loosely. By and large, I have found very little benefit in stereotyping men or women in certain categories, especially in pastoral ministry. I've worked with many men who are highly sensitive, intuitive, and nurturing. I have also worked with women who are competitive, logical, and goal-oriented. I suggest we take people as we find them, seeing every person as worthy of our attention and consideration, just as we would like to be seen ourselves.

Furthermore, I think American readers need to be cautious about not foisting American cultural sensibilities onto their understanding of gender and then insisting on its primacy. As a non-American who doesn't live in the US, I find some of the gender stereotypes commonly assumed by Americans to be glaring. In an interview several years ago for *Relevant Magazine*, Driscoll said:

In Revelation, Jesus is a prize-fighter with a tattoo down His leg, a sword in His hand and the commitment to make someone bleed. That is the guy I can worship. I cannot worship the hippie, diaper, halo Christ because I cannot worship a guy I can beat up.[17]

Maybe Driscoll misspoke on this one, but it's hard to understand why he finds himself unable to worship a guy he could beat up when Jesus was, in effect, crucified by us! He is the Suffering Servant, the Lamb of God, and rather than carrying a sword with "a commitment to make someone bleed," the Jesus of the Gospels willingly chose to suffer and die for his enemies. Furthermore, he commands his followers to do the same.[18] In fact, Jesus makes loving enemies and refusing all violence compulsory for his followers. Loving enemies as Jesus commands, and as the rest of the New Testament teaches,[19] requires that we harness and control our sinful impulses to resort to vengeance and violence rather than indulge them. I recognize that Revelation (to which Driscoll was referring) depicts the risen Christ as King and Conqueror. But he is the most unlikely, grace-filled, peaceable king ever imagined—not the American stereotype of the tattooed, weapon-wielding, cage-fighter many want to make him.

Conforming to stereotypes can lead to unwise decisions. John Piper expressed this scenario:

'Suppose,' I said, 'a couple of you students, Jason and Sarah, were walking to McDonald's after dark. And suppose a man with a knife jumped out of the bushes and threatened you. And suppose Jason knows that Sarah has a black belt in karate and could probably disarm the assailant better than he could. Should he step back and tell her to do it? No. He should step in front of her and be ready to lay down his life to protect her, irrespective of competency. It is written on his soul. That is what manhood does.'[20]

It seems that Sarah should hang back and allow her partner to be stabbed to death, even if she could prevent it, because this is what her gender dictates should be the case. According to Mr. Piper, our God-given gender makeup drives us to make foolhardy choices, "irrespective of competency." In other words, "real men" are constitutionally incapable of having romantic relationships with strong women like Sarah. In this kind of thinking, Christian men are precluded from being the primary caregivers for their children. Women are discouraged from earning more than their spouse earns. All this goes along with the gender stereotype that romance is a "feminine need." Women who want sex without romance are not real women. Men who need romance are not real men. Men who don't need or want sex, well, they don't even exist.

Where does this stuff come from? Not from the Bible. In fact, the Bible is remarkably frank about shattering gender stereotypes. Consider the following:

- David is a sensitive man with a deep and intimate relationship with his friend Jonathan. He writes poetry and music, and has an illicit dalliance at the palace while his troops are fighting for him in the field.

- Gideon is a timid and highly anxious leader who insists that Yahweh continue to satisfy his demand for signs that he will be successful in battle.

- Boaz is reluctant to fulfill the requirements placed upon him as the widowed Ruth's kinsman-redeemer, until she takes matters into her own hands and effectively tricks him into fulfilling those obligations.

- Jeremiah is a melancholic personality who at times can sound niggling and resentful.

Of course, there are examples of "manly" men like Samson, but he is also depicted as petty, cruel, violent, and childish. We also see examples of women who dispel the stereotype. Four strong women appear in Jesus' genealogy:

- Tamar, who impersonated a temple prostitute to trick her father-in-law into providing her with a son (two, in fact)

- Rahab, the Canaanite traitor and prostitute who aided the spies of Joshua

- Ruth, the aforementioned Moabitess who faked a seduction to twist Boaz's arm to do the right thing

- Bathsheba, the victim of a king's seduction (rape?) who schemes to have her son recognized as successor

What they share in common is a willingness to take matters into their own hands. They all sense the precariousness of their positions and decide not to wait and hope for men to act in their interests. They are resolute, decisive, and actional. If Scripture is happy to depict characters that both confirm and shatter stereotypes, so should we.

Promote and Encourage Women Leaders

Some years ago, I spoke at a large outdoor Christian festival. It was an event I was regularly invited to speak at. But one year, I tried something a little different. Accepting the opportunity to speak, I invited one of my students, Linda Axelsson, to share the platform with me. She was a young woman from Sweden who had completed several internships under my direction and shared my perspective on the topic of the conference. We worked together on writing the presentations, divided the material in two, and co-presented it over three sessions. I was not prepared for the reaction we received. For a start, women in the audience were incredibly impressed to hear another woman's voice on the platform and flocked to talk to Linda after each session. (This is something I've seen happen every time I share the platform with my dear friend and colleague, Debra Hirsch. Women mob her after she speaks, not only grateful for the content of her presentations, but thankful for her very presence.) Furthermore, both men and women thanked me for creating the space for them to hear Linda's insights.

It might sound patronizing to suggest that men should be responsible for creating this space for women's voices, but until churches and Christian conferences start offering such opportunities, it might be incumbent upon those of us whose voices are already respected to fashion such partnerships. It is also our responsibility to ensure that women are offered places on teams, committees, and think-tanks, so that their insights and contributions can be adequately made. This will involve a concerted effort from those of us who currently exercise influence in this field.

Conclusion

Isn't this conversation all a little redundant when women hold positions as the heads of Yahoo! and Nike, the immediate past US Secretary of State, the COO of Facebook, the head of the International Monetary Fund, the vice chair of Ernst & Young, and the heads of state of Germany, Australia, Malawi, Korea, Kosovo, Brazil, Iceland, Thailand, Denmark, Switzerland, Jamaica, Costa Rica, Lithuania, Argentina and Liberia?

Women are extremely effective communicators, capable of making insightful observations about their congregations, using what they discover to direct, coach, and develop others. Women build community, searching for ways to unify and build strong congregations. They foster a great sense of belonging, which encourages loyalty. They strive for building consensus, focusing on win-win outcomes that unite people and activate them to contribute at more inspired levels. It is proven that women are the world's most effective collaborators. They are aware that the collective contributions of an organization are greater than those by isolated superstars or soloists. Women value others' emotions, ideas, and humanity; this emotional connection bonds them with their teams and inspires loyalty, commitment, and sacrifice.

I say this without making any comparison or reference to male leadership. Women can be exceptional leaders and teachers. We are poorer for the lack of their voice in our midst.

Discussion Questions

1. The author suggests five ways to affirm the roles of women in leadership. Which one do you find yourself doing on a regular basis?

2. Which of the five do you find most challenging?

3. Are there any of the five you would choose to never do? Why or why not?

Chapter 15 Notes

1. Dr. Frost has written or edited 13 books, the most recent of which are popular and award-winning. These include: Alan Hirsch and Michael Frost, *The Shaping of Things to Come: Innovation and Mission for the 21st-Century Church*, (Ada: Baker Books, 2003); Michael Frost, *Exiles: Living Missionally in a Post-Christian Culture*, (Ada: Baker Books, 2006); and Michael Frost, *The Road to Missional: Journey to the Center of the Church*, (Ada: Baker Books, 2011).

2. Ranke-Heinemann, Uta. *Eunuchs for the Kingdom of Heaven*, (New York: Doubleday, 1990), 122.

3. Ibid., 187-189.

4. Ellen T. Charry, *By the Renewing of Your Minds: The Pastoral Function of Christian Doctrine*, (New York: Oxford University Press, 1999).

5. Sarah Coakley, *Faith, Rationality and the Passions*, (Hoboken: Wiley-Blackwell, 2012).

6. Rachel Held Evans, *Evolving in Monkey Town: How a Girl Who Knew All the Answers Learned to Ask the Questions*, (Grand Rapids, Zondervan, 2010), and *A Year of Biblical Womanhood*, (Nashville, Thomas Nelson Publishers, 2012).

7. Jen Hatmaker, *7: An Experimental Mutiny Against Excess,* (Nashville, B&H Books, 2012).

8. Carolyn Custis James, *Half the Church: Recapturing God's Global Vision for Women,* (Grand Rapids, Zondervan, 2011).

9. Alan and Debra Hirsch, *Untamed: Reactivating a Missional Form of Discipleship,* (Ada: Baker Books, 2010).

10. Ann Morisy, *Bothered and Bewildered: Enacting Hope in Troubled Times,* (New York: Bloomsbury Academic, 2009).

11. Nancey Murphy, *Bodies and Souls, or Spirited Bodies?* (Cambridge: Cambridge University Press, 2006).

12. Jo Saxton, *Real God, Real Life: Finding a Spirituality That Works,* (London: Hodder and Stoughton, 2010).

13. Kathryn Tanner, *Christ the Key,* (Cambridge: Cambridge University Press, 2010); and *Jesus, Humanity and the Trinity,* (Minneapolis: Fortress Press, 2001).

14. David Murrow, *Why Men Hate Going to Church,* (Nashville, Thomas Nelson, 2011), 74.

15. Brandon O'Brien, "A Jesus for Real Men," *Christianity Today,* April 2008, http://www.christianitytoday.com/ct/2008/april/27.48.html.

16. "Why Men Stay Away From the Feminized Church," *Wintery Night,* March 2009, http://winteryknight.wordpress.com/2009/03/11/why-men-stay-away-from-the-feminized-church/.

17. "From the Mag: 7 Big Questions," *Relevant Magazine,* August 2007, http://www.relevantmagazine.com/god/church/features/1344-from-the-mag-7-big-questions.

18. For example: Matthew 5:43-45; Luke 6:27-36.

19. For example: Romans 12:14; Romans 12:17-21; 1 Peter 2:21-23.

20. John Piper, "Co-ed Combat and Cultural Cowardice," *Desiring God,* November 2007, http://www.desiringgod.org/resource-library/taste-see-articles/co-ed-combat-and-cultural-cowardice.

DIANA GAINES and her husband, Kip, have worked side by side since 1983 as a ministry team with YWAM, a large mission-sending organization. They teach team development, discipleship, and pastoral care, and take ministry teams all over the world to serve local, practical needs. Some of their adventures were like living pages out of National Geographic. Although both are heavily involved with those they disciple, Kip and Diana keep their relationship with the Lord first. Marriage and family are also high priorities (four children, two grandchildren). They certainly face challenges, but not with power struggles or authority issues. Kip and Diana's priority is obedience, even when God leads them simultaneously in different directions. They have learned to respect what the other hears from God. They embrace both their unique leadership gifting and calling as a team. At one point, Diana spent a year totally sidelined with a brain bleed, and it took about 10 years to feel "normal" again. She refused to allow this to hinder the call on her life. Her intimacy with Christ plunged her deeper, and God broadened their influence by giving her a fresh understanding of his love and prophetic purposes for the nation of Israel. They are currently based out of both Texas and the Middle East.

CHAPTER 16

BEAUTY AND STRENGTH

Julie Ross

One of the advantages of women and men co-laboring together is that they bring different attributes and gifts to the table. The synergy comes in the diversity. With a few contextual exceptions, an all-male team or project is weaker for not having a feminine voice and vice versa. While it's obviously a generalization, perhaps the female contributions to the partnership can be summarized as "beauty," and the male as "strength." There is something very engaging about the idea of beauty and strength cooperating together. While either can function without the other, our combined efforts carry greater weight and better express the fullness of the body of Christ. Let's work together, embracing our differences.

As a disciple, teacher, and leader, Julie Ross has thought much about this through the years. Here are some of her reflections.

Ya gotta start somewhere…

I went to university in the mid-1970s, and one of my majors was broadcasting. In that era, there were few female radio announcers. At my first job, I was the first woman "voice" they had ever hired, making me a bit of a novelty. I then joined the broadcast team of a startup regional Christian radio station and was their first female broadcaster. My role quickly grew from early-morning-drive news and banter to developing all sorts of ministry components. I hosted a weekly interview show, developed a live prayer/devotional ministry, and hosted a fair amount of listener call-in programming. I only worked part-time, but I enjoyed it all and ministered to a five-state region. It was great to work with men who respected me and my work.

This evolved into a fair amount of public speaking at events and retreats. All the while, I partnered with my husband, a non-denominational pastor, in raising our four sons. I vividly remember the day I laid down two babes to nap and they wondrously slept at the same time, so I had a few minutes to myself. I pulled out a dusty shoebox of scribbled notes and referenced research I had casually gleaned for years on various women throughout history. These women weren't necessarily famous themselves, but had mothered children who grew up to be transformational change agents. I longed to write their stories. And, for the record, I also longed to serve and minister in the nations, but I had my hands full as a pastor's wife, part-time employee, and mom to four squirmy boys. Deep down, I felt God had other assignments for me. I surrendered my life to God afresh and remember thinking, *Are all these desires from you? Or is it just me?*

Many women know they have a call of God on their lives. But one of the cultural and spiritual issues that has hamstrung the body of Christ for centuries is the value and role of a woman. As a created race, we have been schizophrenic through the ages on how we have regarded "her"—from country to country, from generation to generation, from religion to religion, and (regrettably) from Christian church to Christian church.

Some years ago, while serving on a US board of directors for an international, non-governmental organization, we visited Afghanistan to check on some of our projects. As the only woman on the board, I was instructed to walk behind my male American co-workers when we were out and about on the streets, in keeping with the cultural norm. It felt strange to navigate in a subservient posture, missing out on the conversation. As I followed along, I reflected on the deep and dark emotional baggage a whole country of women must experience with this pervasive and demeaning mentality. And to boot, my dear friends didn't even notice the indignity I experienced (felt) when a passing Afghan man catcalled me and pinched me on the behind.

The tables turned when we drove to one of our rural sites, and one of my fellow co-leaders opened the door for me and helped me out of the vehicle onto a rough, rocky construction site. Some of the national Afghan men who were waiting watched us with gaping mouths, aghast at this gender courtesy. One of them even asked via a translator who I could possibly be that a man would treat me with such honor. Was I a president?

A potent observation was made by a female missionary:

It would seem that there is an unwritten rule that goes like this: 'A woman must never, never ever have spiritual authority over a man unless that man lives in a remote part of the world and has skin at least two shades darker than her own.'[1]

Ouch.

God has chosen to use men and women of obedience together throughout the centuries to fulfill his purposes. In the very beginning God said, "It's not good for man to be alone."[2] Woman was created as his ideal counterpart. We were given the mandate from Eden as a team—to be fruitful and multiply, to use the earth's resources and be a blessing to it.[3]

We are, in essence, a spirit species. In Christ, there is no male or female. A male soul has no more value than a female soul; we are all one in Christ.[4] He poured out his Holy Spirit on men and women alike—all flesh.[5] And the generous Holy Spirit gives spiritual gifts as he wills;[6] absolutely none of these gifts are gender-specific. We have all been given the same charge: "Go, and make disciples of all nations."[7] Where and how is by personal assignment. We all have full access to what was purchased on the cross.

God himself has both masculine and feminine attributes. Just as much as he is El Shaddai (the breasty one) and God of all comfort, he is Abba (daddy, papa), and Everlasting Father. And amazingly, we are his image bearers. We are his body and we need each other.

Elke Werner, senior associate for the Lausanne Committee for World Evangelization, offers this:

> In the body of Christ, we all serve together. No part can be left out, no part is more important, and no part is independent of the others. No part only leads; no part only submits. All receive and give at the same time. Christ himself is the only head.[8]

David Fitch says it this way:

> Equality is based on mutual participation. It's not an equality that obliterates our differences.[9]

So men and women get to work together—because God said so.

DNA and Uniqueness

Only one chromosome separates male from female, which doesn't seem like much. But in DNA-speak, the difference is striking. According to Christian authors Walt and Barbara Larimore, male and female brains are dramatically different anatomically, chemically, hormonally, and physiologically. These differences cause fundamentally different ways of thinking, feeling, and behaving, as this article by author, speaker, and entrepreneur Joanna L. Krotz explains:

> Researchers are discovering physiological variations in the brains of men and women. For example, male brains are about 10% larger than female brains. But women have more nerve cells in certain areas. Women also tend to have a larger corpus callosum—the group of nerve fibers that connects left and right hemispheres. That makes women faster at transferring data between the computational, verbal left half and the intuitive, visual right half. Men are usually left-brain oriented.[10]

And how do these unique distinctions play out? Permit me to generalize a bit. Men are hunters. They tend to be directive and hierarchical. The male orientation tends to be highly systemized, even compartmentalized. Males have greater abilities to control emotion, are more aggressive, and tend to compete with other males.

By contrast, women are gatherers. The female orientation is collaborative, relational, nurturing, cooperative, tends to the welfare of others, and seeks the common good. Females are more cautionary, able to multitask, and have a lower ability to compartmentalize or control emotion.

So, we are male and female, and in God's economy, co-equal. We are unique and interdependent in design. We're on the same team.

Good Foundations

But in order to function optimally together, certain things are needful. For one, be fully committed to your own personal growth. I like this statement: "Whatever you are, be a good one."[11] Through a biblical lens, lifetime success has more to do with character and holiness than it does with skill and knowledge. Christian philosopher, Dallas Willard, is frequently quoted as saying, "What God gets out of me isn't what I do, it's the person I become." True personal godliness comes from inner transformation. And, as the saying goes, "it don't come cheap."

Carolyn Custis James is an author, speaker, and leader, known for her biblical and affirming encouragement for Kingdom women. At a conference, she is quoted as saying:

As an image bearer of God, you can't know who you are or what your purpose is if you don't know the One you're supposed to be becoming like. There's a studied passivity that we get into when we believe that God has called only men to leadership. I don't think you can be an image bearer and not be called to leadership. That may take a lot of different forms, but oh my goodness, what a big deal that is.[12]

As the adage says—know thyself. In the context of real-time spiritual disciplines, discover and mature yourself in your spiritual gifts.[13] Modern-day tools like Meyers-Briggs, StrengthsFinder, DISC, and Love Languages can foster self-discovery and potentially nourish confidence, sharpen focus, and enhance richness in ministry. The more we learn about how we (and others) tick, the more we can lower the fence between us, and the easier it is for truth to pass between us.

Commit to Excellence in Interpersonal Communication

Interpersonal (face-to-face) communication includes messages we send through our facial expressions, body language, tone of voice, and gestures. We can all probably recall an incident where we felt either demeaned or judged, honored or valued—with nary a word spoken.

Thirty years ago, a businessperson was generally hired on the basis of technical skills. Today, Fortune 500 companies name strong interpersonal, communication, and team skills as the most important criteria for success in management positions.[14]

Active listening is likely the most important component of an interpersonal skillset, but it takes intentionality, time, and patience to master. We don't need to be agreed with, but if we are not even listened to, with value and weight connected to our sharing—well, that's just downright disrespectful. What kind of a listener are you?[15]

I believe a steady diet of exclusively male contribution to a group, team, board, or body, can leave the big picture potentially sterile and lacking in dimension. A steady diet of exclusively female representation can lack in formation and strategy. Perhaps the full-orbed blending of outward and inward, cerebral and feeling, fact and intuition, and strength and beauty, contributes to the construction of an even healthier team. And that means choosing to walk in grace and honor, deferring to each other—whether as partners in a healthy marriage or working together in some other context.

Female Ambitions and Leadership Contributions

In the USA between 1997 and 2007, the number of businesses owned by women grew by 44 percent, twice as fast as those owned by men. The number of women who lead non-profits steadily increases every year.[16] According to a December 2012 interview on ABC news, women now comprise 50 percent of the workforce, 70 percent of the degrees, 51 percent of the nation's PhDs, 51 percent of business school applicants, 67 percent of college graduates, and more than 70 percent of 2012 valedictorians.

McKinsey & Company is self-described as an international management consulting firm that helps leading corporations and organizations make distinctive, lasting, and substantial improvements in their performance. They offer research regarding leadership behaviors that men and women bring to management teams and suggest that increased gender diversity and female leadership at the corporate level is of strategic importance. One of their studies found that men and women rank equally in intellectual stimulation and efficient communication, but noted differences in leadership style. Prevalent male leadership behaviors included control, corrective action, and individualistic decision-making. Common female leadership behaviors focused on people development, expectations and rewards, being a role model, inspiration, and participative decision-making. The report says this:

> Women leaders are more persuasive, assertive, and more willing to take risks than male leaders. Women leaders were found to be more empathetic and flexible, as well as stronger in interpersonal skills than their male counterparts. These qualities combine to create a leadership style that is inclusive, open, consensus building, collaborative, and collegial. (paraphrase)[17]

Research from the London Business School has shown, in the areas of experimentation, efficiency, and psychological safety, the optimal balance for teams is a 50-50 mix of men and women, whereas a 60 percent female, 40 percent male mix creates the optimal conditions for team confidence.[18] Companies who take the lead in strategic gender diversity are said to have a clear advantage on success margins.[19]

Research has since made it abundantly clear that context makes a critical difference. Women face the most resistance to their leadership and influence in roles that are male-dominated and characterized as masculine. As social attitudes have shifted to define fewer arenas as masculine, acceptance of women as leaders in the other arenas has grown.[20]

An interview study of women leaders in France and Norway illustrated years ago that context could make all the difference to these leaders' experiences. In Norway, with its long and deeply rooted history of women's involvement in political leadership, women in such positions felt a strong sense of legitimacy in their leadership roles. In France, where women's leadership was relatively new and rare, that sense of legitimacy was absent, and the women were called upon to prove themselves repeatedly. The Norwegian women expressed joy and a sense of efficacy in their leadership roles; the French women spoke of difficulties, conflicts, loneliness, and marginality. These differing experiences appear linked to sharp contrasts in these women's perceptions of their acceptance as leaders.[21]

What about Kingdom Women?

As we look to the church of the twenty-first century and our call to be salt and light in the context of a post-modern, post-Christian culture, what style of leadership can take us forward most fruitfully? Many believe relational leadership trumps hierarchical leadership.

Just imagine what could happen in his Kingdom if we were strategic in maximizing each gender's strengths. In business, the bottom line is financial profit. For us, isn't it building his Kingdom?

It's important that the church's senior leaders take initiative on the gender issue by supporting women. What the senior pastor believes about women forms the template for church function and determines how authority flows. What do the decision makers assume about those who comprise half the body of Christ where you worship?

Nineteenth-century revivalist Charles Finney is an example of a ministry leader who invited women to pray and speak in public worship. He founded Oberlin College, the first college in America to allow women to study alongside men (and the first college to be racially integrated). Finney was also the first Protestant leader to train women in theology, and his student, Antoinette Brown, became the first woman ordained in America.[22]

Fast forward to 2007. An organization called Christians for Biblical Equality conducted research to learn how many current denominations affirm women in leadership. Of 64 denominations, 21 affirmed women in leadership, 13 were unclear, and 30 did not.[23]

Evidence of Change?

According to George Barna's research, no population group among the 60 segments he examined has gone through more spiritual changes in the past two decades than women. One study found that after decades of zero growth in the number of female senior pastors of Protestant churches, women have made substantial gains in the past years, rising from five percent to 10 percent. I imagine some of you are thrilled at the progress; some of you lament it's not higher.

Another conclusion from Barna's research: "Women in the pulpit are generally more highly educated than are their male counterparts."[24] At many Bible colleges, more than half the student population is female. Doesn't it strike you a little bit like being all dressed up and nowhere to go? You may find it interesting that single women outnumber single men 4:1 on the mission field.

Creating Space

What can we do to create more space for women to obey what they are called to do? Shall we give reluctant mental assent but never really champion our women—wives, daughters, sisters in Christ? Or shall we be supportive in every possible way? Everybody wins when we cheer women on, help them develop their capacities, create networking opportunities for them, and power them forward.

The Assemblies of God denomination ordains women. Many of their churches have female pastors or a gender mix within their leadership. The denomination offers a website called The Network—A Called Community of Women. Here's a sampling of comments from men and women who serve side by side in vocational ministry:[25]

> Sometimes males and females view things differently. A staff with both men and women allows us to bring different perspectives to issues and to play off each other's strengths.

> It brings balance. And that's important in the church because we are ministering to so many fractured families that don't see healthy male-female relationships. We need a strong male-female ministry model to show them what that looks like.

> I have found that my female staff 'raise the bar' of excellence. They have consistently been hard workers, good with detail, and also discerning. My experience has been that the staff is stronger and more balanced when it includes both men and women.

> Both men and women have strengths that complement each other. In our church, we even rotate the preaching among the staff members. That allows people in the congregation to relate to different styles of preaching and different personalities of pastors. It also provides role models for the people.

Don't waste time feeling threatened or being competitive with the other gender. If you feel threatened, it's either a real threat and you need to do something about it, or it's an ego issue and you need to get over it.

Besides, who gets the glory for it all? Patrick S. Franklin, referencing Gordon Fee, writes this:

Ministry is not primarily a human accomplishment but a response to the ministry of the triune God. Specifically, redeemed people minister out of their union with Christ in the bond of the Spirit, not on the basis of gender or any other innate quality.[26]

Jesus is not our problem. And neither are the words of the Apostle Paul. The enemy has operated on an agenda throughout millennia. Perhaps the most foreboding "giant in the land" may be the one who is looking back at us in the mirror—whichever gender we are. It takes disarming honesty to root out our own mindsets that have become strongholds, whether they have been inherited from others, come from a wounded place, or just plain don't stand the test of biblical integrity.

And there you have it: the beauty, synergy, and power of *Missio Dei* (the mission of God). A couple things I do know: one, a daughter has no greater ally than a Father who believes in her; and two, there is simply too much at stake to not utilize all who are equipped.

Many years ago, George Otis, founder of The Sentinel Group and producer of the *Transformation* videos, stayed at our home while he was doing research for a video project. I have come to honor the depth of his research, so it was with great interest that I read about his visit to the Outer Hebrides (off the West coast of Scotland) to meet with survivors of the remarkable Hebrides revival of the early 1950s. He met with the now-elderly folk in small groups, sometimes for hours at a time. They were exceedingly polite and sober, with one notable exception. When George asked questions about God's Spirit falling on them, group members would just start weeping. This happened consistently with each group he met.[27]

We can quibble and divide about things like who can teach and when, and who can lead and under what circumstances. But when God's Spirit falls, and he comes in power, all else pales by contrast and falls by the wayside. His presence, his glory—this is our prize. May God grant us the grace to keep first things first, judge the part by the whole, hunger for his glory alone, and practice genuine gratefulness for the privilege of co-laboring together in his vineyards.

Discussion Questions

1. What do you think about the generalizations made about men and women in this chapter?

2. What synergistic effects might result in your faith community from having men and women co-laboring together? Is there anything to prevent this from happening?

3. Share how you see each other being used to build God's Kingdom.

Chapter 16 Notes

1. "Single Lady Missionaries," *Stuff Fundies Like,* accessed January 2014, http://www.stufffundieslike.com/2008/12/single-lady-missionaries.
2. Genesis 2:18.
3. Genesis 1:28.
4. Galatians 3:28.
5. Acts 2:17-18.
6. 1 Corinthians 12.
7. Matthew 28:18-20.
8. Elke Werner, "Reconciliation of God: Men and Women Working Together," *Lausanne World Pulse,* May 2009, http://www.lausanneworldpulse.com/themedarticles.php/1141?pg=all.
9. David Fitch, "Woman and Men in Ministry Together: Affirming Women and Transforming – The Missional Way," *Reclaiming the Mission,* March 2010, http://www.reclaimingthemission.com/?p=1007.
10. Joanna L. Krotz, "Why Women Make Better Managers," accessed January 2014, http://www.eng.utoledo.edu/mime/faculty_staff/faculty/rbennett/womenmanagers.htm.

11. Attributed to Abraham Lincoln.

12. Amy Simpson and Ginger Kolbaba, "God's Purpose for Women," *Today's Christian Woman*, November 2009, http://www.todayschristianwoman. com/articles/2009/november-issue/gods-purpose-for-women.html.

13. These gifts are listed in 1 Corinthians 12 and Romans 12.

14. "Interpersonal Communications," accessed January 2009, http://business. uni.edu/buscomm/Interpersonal/InterpersonalCommunication.htm.

15. Find more at: http://www.skillsyouneed.co.uk/IPS/active_listening. html#ixzz2EqXndaEo.

16. "Women-Owned Businesses in the 21st Century," U.S. Department of Commerce Economics and Statistics Administration, October 2010, http://www. esa.doc.gov/sites/default/files/reports/documents/women-owned-businesses.pdf.

17. "Women Matter: Gender Diversity, A Corporate Performance Driver," McKinsey & Company, 2007, http://www.mckinsey.com/features/ women_matter.

18. "Innovative Potential: Men and Women in Teams," London Business School, accessed January 2014, http://www.20-first.com/1612-0-innovative-potential--men-and-women-in-teams.html.

19. http://www.mckinsey.com/locations/paris/home/womenmatter/pdfs/ women_matter_oct2008_english.pdf.

20. Hilary Lips, *A New Psychology of Women: Gender, Culture and Ethnicity*, (Houston: Mayfield Publishing Company, 1999).

21. This information can be found at http://onlinelibrary.wiley.com/ doi/10.1111/j.1471-6402.1993.tb00653.x/abstract.

22. Loren Cunnigham and David J. Hamilton, *Why Not Women? A Fresh Look at Scripture on Women in Missions, Ministry and Leadership*, (Seattle: YWAM Publishing, 2000), 25.

23. "US Denominations and Their Stances on Women in Leadership," CBE, April 2007, http://www2.cbeinternational.org/new/E-Journal/2007/07spring/ denominations%20first%20installment--FINAL.pdf.

24. Barna Group, September 2009, http://www.barna.org/leadership-articles/304-number-of-female-senior-pastors-in-protestant-churches-doubles-in-past-decade.

25. http://womeninministry.ag.org/resources/interviews/intrv_0703_ maleandfemale.cfm.

26. Patrick S. Franklin (referencing Gordon Fee), "Women Sharing in the Ministry of God: A Trinitarian Framework for the Priority of Spirit Gifting as a Solution to the Gender Debate," *Priscilla Papers*, Autumn 2008, http:// www.academia.edu/3136066/Women_Sharing_in_the_Ministry_of_ God_A_Trinitarian_Framework_for_the_Priority_of_Spirit_Gifting_as_a_ Solution_to_the_Gender_Debate.

27. George Otis Jr., "Why Revival Tarries… in America," *Charisma Magazine*, November 2012, 43.

EPILOGUE
WE HAVE A DREAM...

By Felicity Dale

All it took was one. One black swan to disprove the well-known "fact" that swans are always white. Similarly with women in the Kingdom, all it takes is one. One Deborah, one Esther, one Priscilla, one Phoebe, one Junia. One woman whom God has called to lead and save nations or to lead in the church. One woman to prove that God doesn't place limits on women. This tribe of black swans—women whom God has empowered to change nations or transform society—exists not only in the Scriptures, but also down through the pages of history to the present day.

Through the centuries, men have led in ways that relate to traditionally male strengths. They have dominated and controlled; they have fought for prominence, position, and fame; they have become rivals in competing for the largest church building, the greatest number of members, the biggest budget.

As women, we can choose to demonstrate a different way. As God releases us, we have some choices. We can decide that we should defend our rights as women—rights to position and authority, to status, to our place on the platform. Or we can choose a better way—the way of the cross—laying down our lives in service for others. We've had centuries of practice. Let's willingly embrace a life of humility.

Most of today's female disciples of Jesus are not competing for position or recognition; they are content to remain nameless and faceless. All they want is to follow Jesus, loving him, listening to his voice, obeying his call on their lives. And for some of them, that call includes fulfilling roles that are traditionally associated with men.

In the workforce, many women occupy responsible positions. They make decisions, implement projects, and are having an impact on their world. But they long to use their gifts and talents in the one place (after home and family) that means the most to them—the body of Christ.

What we believe matters. It makes a difference in our attitudes, in our thought processes, in our actions, and in the way we treat other people. What we believe about women matters. It determines their role in the Kingdom of God. If we believe God has created women to follow men, many will continue to sit passively on the sidelines, waiting for men to take the initiative and supporting them as best they can. But if we believe God has given women the freedom to go beyond this, we will see more women boldly step out in faith to answer his call, embrace their strength in him, and carry out great exploits—just like the women we've profiled in this book. And we will see a harvest of souls as a result.

God is releasing a fresh understanding of the Scriptures that have been used in the past to limit women's roles. As women learn that those Scriptures can be understood, with integrity, to mean something very different, they can feel released to stop being passive followers. They might long to get more active in the Kingdom, to create initiatives, to labor in the harvest. If women are not fully included, they will likely take their giftings elsewhere (much like the apostolic men and women who started para-church organizations when they weren't given freedom to express their talents within the church). That would be a tragedy.

But there's another possible scenario. If, as Peggy Batcheller-Hijar suggests in her chapter, it takes an "immense thrust" to create a movement, then working together, we can change the attitude of the church toward women.

What might happen if women rise up, not in rebellion, but in determination to obey Jesus rather than conform to tradition, no matter the cost? What might happen if they refuse to be bound by convention and follow the Holy Spirit as he leads them, not hindered by constraints of "but a woman isn't allowed to do this"? What if they felt free to initiate missional or social projects without having to wait for permission? What if they acted as role models for a younger generation who will not tolerate the kind of gender bias the church has shown in the past? What if they came as equal co-laborers for the Kingdom in their own right, able to use their gifts and talents in the service of their King?

What might happen if men opened the doors for women? What might happen if they chose to ignore the frowns of their peers and include women on their teams—not as a token female representation, but as equals with the men? What if they welcomed and valued the diversity of the more feminine gifts of spiritual intuition and their ability to forge relationships? What if they gave them responsibility for strategy and development? What if they treated them as equal partners in the work? If they asked them to teach or train others—not only women and children, but the whole body of Christ? What if they sent them out to make disciples—baptizing new believers, teaching them to obey Jesus and starting churches? What if they championed women?

What might happen if men and women labored together in the Kingdom?

That is our dream!

Just think. A whole generation might grow up that has never experienced or practiced gender discrimination.

We already know how the story ends. God's Kingdom come and his will be done, on earth as it is in heaven. The ultimate climactic resolution of history as we know it is that the Kingdom is fully manifested, justice prevails in every domain, and when we are able to see him face-to-face, the Scriptures we cannot currently fully understand will finally become clear.

In that day, when there is a new heaven and earth, there will be no death, no mourning, no crying or pain. Those who have been tortured, humiliated, ignored—those who are poor in spirit—will inherit the Kingdom. Many people, both males and females, will discover their full potential in that day and will be stunned to discover how beautifully and wonderfully made they truly are. Meanwhile though, during these in-between years while we are waiting for goodness to prevail, we are still responsible to work toward justice, help wipe away tears, work arm in arm toward unity in the whole body, and uphold Scripture as best as we possibly can.

May the tribe of black swans increase to the glory of God.

ABOUT THE AUTHORS

This has truly been a team effort. While Felicity has perhaps done more to coordinate the process, everyone has contributed far beyond just writing their chapters. The team of women has had dozens of phone conversations for more than three years. The male contributors have stood with us, encouraged us, promoted us, been "Baraks" in every sense of the word. Here's a little about the authors:

PEGGY BATCHELLER-HIJAR became a committed follower of Jesus at the age of 17. She has always had a heart for missions and church planting here in the US as well as overseas, and has been on various missions trips to several Central and South American countries. She is married to Richard Hijar, and together they minister through organic church settings to men and women throughout New Mexico and Southeast Colorado. She works as a nurse, and is currently is employed as a supervisor in a senior living facility in Albuquerque, New Mexico.

NEIL COLE is an experienced church planter, author, and pastor. He is credited as a key catalyst in the organic church movement and is founder of Church Multiplication Associates (CMA), which has helped to start tens of thousands of churches in 50 states and more than 50 nations in only 14 years. Neil is also an international speaker and has authored many books, including: *Organic Church, Cultivating a Life For God, Organic Leadership, Church 3.0, Journeys to Significance,* and *Primal Fire.*

FELICITY DALE trained as a physician in the UK and moved to the States in 1987. She is best known for her work with house churches around the world. She was one of the founders of House2House Ministries. She writes and blogs frequently about the simple/organic/ church movement, as well as on the topic of women in ministry. Felicity is author of *Getting Started* and *An Army of Ordinary People*. She also co-authored *Small is Big!* with her husband, Tony, and George Barna.

JAN DISS is a minister in a mainline denomination. She is passionate about reproducing new disciples, new ministries, and new churches.

KATIE DRIVER has more than 29 years of experience in church plant-ing, discipleship, leadership training—igniting and equipping people in both the United States and internationally. She is a simple/organic/ missional mentor and coach, and is a trainer for CMA's Greenhouse. Katie and her husband, Tom, have been married 29 years, have three children, and live in Minnesota. She is also an instructor/trainer for the MSF Course (Motorcycle Safety Training), and writes a blog on the journey of simple, organic, and missional life called "Backseat Driver."

DAVE FERGUSON is the Lead Pastor of Community Christian Church, an innovative, multi-site, missional church. He is passion-ate about "helping people find their way back to God." Community has grown from a few college friends to thousands meeting every weekend at 14 locations throughout Chicagoland and has been recognized as one of the most influential churches in America. Dave also provides visionary leadership for NewThing, a catalyst for movements of reproducing churches. He is an award-winning author of books such as *The Big Idea, Exponential, On the Verge* (with Alan Hirsch), and *Discover Your Mission Now.*

MICHAEL FROST is an Australian missiologist based in Sydney, where he heads up the Tinsley Institute, a mission study center. He is also a senior lecturer with the Melbourne University of Divinity. He has written or edited more than a dozen books on such subjects as film, gender studies, Christology, and missiology. His books include *Exiles* and *Road to Missional*. He also co-authored *The Shaping of Things to Come* and *ReJesus* with Alan Hirsch.

ALAN HIRSCH is the founding director of Forge Mission Training Network. Currently, he co-leads Future Travelers, a learning program to help megachurches become missional movements. Known for his innovative approach to mission, Alan is considered a thought-leader and key mission strategist for churches across the Western world. Hirsch is the author of *The Forgotten Ways*, co-author of *The Shaping of Things to Come, ReJesus*, and *The Faith of Leap* (with Michael Frost); *Untamed* (with Debra Hirsch); *Right Here, Right Now* (with Lance Ford); *On the Verge* (with Dave Ferguson); and *The Permanent Revolution* (with Tim Catchim).

LYNNE HYBELS is a freelance author and advocate for global engagement. She started Ten for Congo, a fundraising campaign for victims of war in the Democratic Republic of Congo, hosts educational tours in the Holy Land focused on reconciliation efforts between Israelis and Palestinians, and wrote *Nice Girls Don't Change the World*. In 1975, Lynne and her husband, Bill, started Willow Creek Community Church. Lynne and Bill have two grown children and two grandchildren.

SUZETTE LAMBERT is a licensed marriage and family therapist in the state of Georgia, where she has a private practice. She has been involved in mentoring younger women, having been captivated by youth work in her early 20s. For the last 12 years, she's been involved in a deliverance and inner-healing ministry. She married Robert 33 years ago and they have two grown children. She has written the book *Finding Father*, which addresses relationship with God. She has been involved with home church for the last 10 years.

FLOYD MCCLUNG is the founder and team leader of All Nations, an international movement of churches and church planters. All Nations provides specialized training courses in Kansas City, Missouri; Tainan, Taiwan; and Cape Town, South Africa. Floyd has spoken on more than 100 university campuses and has traveled to 193 countries. He is the author of 14 books, including the best-selling books, *The Father Heart of God, Living on the Devil's Doorstep, Follow* and *You See Bones—I See an Army*.

JULIE ROSS has served in pastoral care ministry both in the US and abroad for many years. Her work in Christian radio broadcasting and speaking has encouraged many. As a wellness and life coach, she loves the power of a good question. She and her husband, Bill, continue to develop their organic farm in South Dakota and cheer on their four adult sons and daughter-in-law.

FRANK VIOLA has helped thousands of people around the world deepen their relationship with Jesus Christ and enter into a more vibrant and authentic experience of church. He has written many books on these themes, including *God's Favorite Place on Earth* and *From Eternity to Here*. His blog, "Beyond Evangelical," is rated one of the most popular in Christian circles today: frankviola.org

JON ZENS has been the editor of *Searching Together* since 1978. He has written many articles and books, including *No Will of My Own: How Patriarchy Smothers Female Dignity* and *Personhood.* Since 1977, he has traveled to small fellowships, encouraging them in Christ-centeredness and conflict resolution. He has a bachelor of arts from Covenant College, an master of divinity from Westminster Seminary, and a doctor of ministry from the California Graduate School of Theology.

Made in the USA
Middletown, DE
18 May 2016